DERBYS
Villages

Text by the Derbyshire Federation of Women's Institutes
Photographs by Bill Meadows

COUNTRYSIDE BOOKS
Newbury, Berkshire

COUNTRYSIDE BOOKS
3 Catherine Road
Newbury, Berkshire

To view our complete range of books,
please visit us at
www.countrysidebooks.co.uk

ISBN 1 85306 748 2

The front cover photograph shows Eyam;
the back cover photograph shows millstones below
Stanage Edge near Hathersage and that on page 4 is of Matlock Bath

Designed by Graham Whiteman

Typeset by Techniset Typesetters, Newton-le-Willows
Produced through MRM Associates Ltd., Reading
Printed in Italy

FOREWORD

Derbyshire is a county of great contrasts, bordered by seven other counties. The most northerly countryside attracts many visitors with its high moorlands of peat, cotton grass, heather and tumbling streams which feed the reservoirs of the upper Derwent Valley. The long gritstone edges which flank the east and western borders enclose a massive limestone plateau studded with unusual rock formations, cliffs, caves and deep wooded gorges, carved over the centuries by the rivers flowing through the county. Continuing southward, the countryside changes to a more lowland pastoral scene.

The county is steeped in history, from ancient stone circles, to Roman settlements, to relics of past industry and the historic houses of Chatsworth, Hardwick, Haddon, Kedleston and Sudbury. To this day agriculture and industry play their part in the continual transformation of the countryside, but the most attractive feature of Derbyshire is its many small villages and their inhabitants.

These are the words of Daphne Irvine, former County Chairman, in her foreword to *The Derbyshire Village Book*, and I cannot better them. This new all-colour volume takes many of the accounts from that book, first published in 1990, and adds superb pictures by landscape photographer Bill Meadows.

We hope that, after reading it, you will feel encouraged to explore for yourself the many small villages and discover the beauty of the Derbyshire countryside.

Barbara Parkinson
County Chairman
Derbyshire Federation of Women's Institutes
Autumn 2002

The Alport Stone

⌘ ALPORT

The Portway, the ancient trackway from Nottingham to Castleton, passes through Alport over the ancient packhorse bridge, and through the ages there will have been a tremendous variety of travellers along this route. Today the hamlet of Alport, where the river Lathkill cascades over limestone waterfalls and weirs to join the more sedate river Bradford, is much visited and admired by anglers, walkers and naturalists. But the present peace and serenity are in sharp contrast to the industrialisation and activity of former times. Alport was among the most bustling of the lead mining villages in the 17th, 18th and 19th centuries, and in the 17th and 18th centuries there were a number of water wheels. However, in the 19th century, the area was unrivalled in its use of water pressure engines developed by Richard Trevithick, and by 1848 six engines were at work for the Alport Mining Company.

Cupola, the lead smelting works built about 1840, provided work which was anything but healthy. Fanny Needham born in 1847 and Alport's oldest inhabitant when the Youlgreave WI compiled an historical record in 1931, is quoted as saying 'the flues were cleaned out twice a year when the men had to have nose and mouth covered and to keep special clothes on shelves at the works. At dinner time all was spoon meat, broth or Irish stew or a posset in winter because they might not touch the food with their hands.'

⌘ ASHFORD-IN-THE-WATER

Artists out of number have trodden the well worn path to Ashford's picturesque and ancient Sheep Wash Bridge. Sheep were washed there until recent times: the lambs would be penned within the stone-walled pen on one side of the river whilst their mothers were thrown in at the other side. They would naturally swim across to their offspring, thus ensuring a good soaking. Originally a medieval packhorse bridge it now attracts hundreds of visitors each year.

The people of Ashford still pay homage to the abundance of water by 'dressing' the six wells every year, in the old Peak District fashion of layering petals, leaves and other natural objects into a bed of clay. The hordes of visitors who pour into Ashford around Trinity Sunday each year bear witness to the high standard of these impressive pictures.

The village church of the Holy Trinity houses the relics of another ancient custom, the funeral garlands suspended from the roof. They were made from white paper, cut to form rosettes and were fixed to a wooden frame. They would be carried before the coffin of a young girl in the funeral procession. This practice was accorded only to virgins. The garland would then be hung in the church. There are four garlands still hanging there, the oldest believed to have been made in 1747.

The well known Ashford marble was first quarried in 1748 by Henry Watson. It

Sheepwash Bridge over the River Wye, Ashford

is not strictly speaking a true marble but an impure limestone. When polished, the black marble provided a perfect background for mosaic and inlaid patterns. Amongst other things it was used for vases, clocks and jewellery. A wonderful example of an inlaid table top is in Ashford church.

⌘ ASHOVER

Essovre is the name which first appeared in the Domesday Book, and is derived from 'the village standing beyond the edge of the ash forest'. Today it is known as Ashover and has been called 'the valley of silence and wild flowers'. The parish is now the second largest in England, far removed from its humble beginnings when in the Domesday Book the record told of a village with 14 smallholders, a church, a priest and an inn.

Many local people were employed by the lead mines and folklore tells us that one famous character was Dorothy Matly, a lady with the dubious reputation of being a 'curser, a liar, and a thief', Hardly surprising then, when a young miner lost twopence it was she who came under suspicion. This she hotly denied, with a dramatic protestation that if she had taken the money the ground would open and swallow her up. The ground did open and the miner retrieved his money.

Butt's Grange is reputed to have been the place where arrows for the battle of

Pear Tree Farm in the Amber Valley

Agincourt were made. And a tree standing nearby is called The Gospel Tree because, according to local tradition, John Wesley preached under it.

The fine church of All Saints dates back to 1350. Inside are the alabaster tomb of the Babington family, the rood screen and one of the few lead fonts left in the country, where babies are still christened today.

⌘ ASTON-UPON-TRENT

The village of Aston-upon-Trent, consisting of 1,793 acres, lies six miles south-east of Derby at the point where the river Trent divides the counties of Derbyshire and Leicestershire. Traces of Saxon pottery were found by the canal and there is Norman tooling on the fine Saxon church. A mound in a nearby field is thought to be an ancient burial ground.

A market cross stood near the stocks on the village green and it was here, in the early 19th century, that charities were distributed to the poor. Other charities included gifts of land, education in the cottage school for one boy and one girl, and for four almshouses to be built. A village pump, though no longer in use, still stands in the centre of the village and the local magazine takes its name from this feature.

Documents of the late 19th century show tradesmen of every kind in the village:

lace and stocking makers, wheelwrights, boot makers, maltsters, bakers, builders, butchers, farmers, rat catchers, constables, innkeepers, tailors, dressmakers, coal merchants, a schoolmaster and a blacksmith whose descendants still reside here.

The beautiful Aston Lodge was then residence of the Bowden family, lace manufacturers. They enjoyed friendly rivalry with the occupiers of the Hall to see who could give the best parties. One of Bowden's daughters, for her marriage, had red carpet laid from the Lodge to the altar steps, some 400 ft. The house was eventually taken down and shipped to America, the stables were converted into flats and the grounds into sports and playing fields.

⌘ BAKEWELL

Up to about the 10th century the river Wye at Bakewell was crossed by using either the Lum Ford, the Bakewell Ford or the Beeley Ford. These river crossings were at

The river Wye through Bakewell

the sites of Holme Bridge, the town bridge at the end of Bridge Street, and the iron bridge near Granby Croft.

The present Holme Bridge dates from 1664 and has five segmental and two semi-circular arches. Its narrowness and the comparatively low parapets identify it as constructed for packhorses whose panniers would overhang the sides. The cutwaters at river level are carried up to form refuges. Packhorses usually travelled in 'trains' of up to 40, and the most common early loads for long distance transport were salt, malt, wool or cheese.

Bakewell Bridge, with five pointed arches, is much older, 13th century, and although it was widened in the 19th century it was probably cart width originally.

The first Bakewell pudding was created during the 19th century, and was the result of a misunderstanding between the mistress of the Rutlands Arms inn, Mrs Greaves, and her cook. On a day when important visitors were expected at the inn for dinner, Mrs Greaves instructed her cook how she wished the pastry made for a strawberry tart; the egg mixture was to be mixed into the pastry and the strawberry jam spread on top. Mrs Greaves was called away to receive her visitors and the cook either forgot or misunderstood the instruction and poured the egg mixture over the jam instead of mixing it in the pastry and what should have been a tart was now a pudding, went to the oven and thence to the table.

Dinner over, the guests sent for Mrs Greaves and complimented her upon her delicious pudding. Mrs Greaves thought it odd that her tart should be called a pudding and she questioned the cook who confessed what she had done.

⌘ BAMFORD

Bamford village is only a small part of the whole area of the parish, which includes many miles of high moorland. To the north it is bounded by the gritstone edges of Derwent and Bamford, and on the west by the peak of Win Hill. It lies within the Peak District National Park.

Approaching Bamford on the A57 from Sheffield the name 'Cut-throat Bridge' may strike terror into the heart of the traveller. This name was given by local 16th century inhabitants who found a man lying there with many wounds to his face and neck. He was carried to a house nearby and then on to Bamford Hall where he died two days later. In those days this road led down to the village of Ashopton, the river Derwent, and then into Bamford. Now it runs alongside Ladybower Reservoir, whose 504 acre expanse is fringed by steep woodlands and fields. The water mirrors the changes of sky and seasonal colours. The first of three reservoirs was constructed in 1901 in the upper Derwent valley and this was followed by two more, the lowest of which, Ladybower, involved the inundation of the villages of Derwent and Ashopton. On the shore of Ladybower stands a gaunt, empty house, its vacant windows staring over the reservoir. Ginnett House was the home of Miss A. Cotterill until her death in 1990 at the age of 99 years. The house was built by her

The Ladybower Reservoir and Ashopton Viaduct

grandfather in 1880 as the family home, looking down onto Ashopton and its surrounding farmlands until they were submerged by the rising water. Miss Cotterill refused to move out, and so stayed on as a tenant of the water authority for the next 50 years. 'They didn't expect I would live so long, but I'm tough,' said Miss Cotterill. The stable and yard now lie beneath the water which laps at the front garden steps.

⌘ BARLOW

Barlow lies about four miles north-west of Chesterfield. Its recorded history dates back to William the Conqueror who gave it to one of his barons named Ascuit Musard of Honfleur. His grandson adopted the name Jordan de Barley and, in 1586, Peter Barley, the last of the family, died. From then the name changed from Barley to Barlow.

The old houses are built of local stone weathered through the years, as is the church of St Laurence, which is 900 years old. It stands on rising ground in a well-kept, grassy churchyard and has an aura of restful timelessness about it. Not far from it is the Methodist chapel.

The great annual event is Well-Dressing Week, when three wells are beautifully decorated. They are done in the form of triptych pictures which are very colourfully composed of whole flower-heads (as against the more usual petals) and other natural materials such as bark and grasses. On the third Wednesday in August an early evening service is held in the flower-filled church and this is followed by a procession through the village to each well, where another brief blessing takes place. There is a tradition that this dates back as far as 1615 when, in spite of a serious drought, the wells managed to supply some water; but its origin is most probably a pagan rite of propitiation to a water god or goddess.

⌘ BASLOW

Down the centuries the village has been closely linked with the Duke of Devonshire's glorious Chatsworth House and parkland, being only two miles

At Baslow in the Derwent Valley

from the centre of the village. Visitors and villagers alike can enjoy this delightful short walk across the park with its wonderful variety of trees, so lovely in every season of the year, and the deer herd, always a good reason to pause and admire them and the surrounding hills.

The church, St Anne's, stands picturesquely at the side of the river Derwent, Derbyshire's longest and most important river, which in years gone by provided water power for the cornmill at nearby Calver.

During the 1880s the Baslow Hydro, known in full as the Baslow Hydropathic Establishment, was built. This proved immensely popular with the more well-to-do businessmen and their families who travelled from the cities to 'take the cure' of Baslow's water. The Hydro continued until the 1920s but is no longer in existence.

The great bleak and desolate moorlands lie to the north and east of the village, in sharp contrast to the evergreen quieter beauty of Chatsworth. An excerpt from one of the early brochures of the Baslow Hydro is as true today as when it was first written: 'If you look at a map of England you will see that Baslow occupies a central position. This is significant, for here, in the heart of England, is to be found the very essence of our country. River and pasture and parkland, green turf and noble trees, wild moors and woods, where in spring bluebells tumble in cascades down the hillsides; grey crags and green dales that hold the secret of beauty in their hollows, innumerable footpaths for the pedestrian, and the newer and stately Ducal Palace with its store of priceless treasures.'

⌘ BEELEY

Beeley nestles in the Peak District National Park between the moors and the river Derwent at the southern end of Chatsworth Park. The church of St Anne dates from the 12th century. Tradition, and superstition, require that the bride and groom must not approach by the west gate and must pay coinage to leave by the roped narrow east gate – the wider one being reserved for funerals. In 1785 one lady died on her way to be married!

Burntwood Quarries, formerly the property of Henry Deeley and now closed, produced a fine quality, weather-resistant gritstone, much of which was used in the construction of Manchester, as well as locally to make grindstones.

The road system was altered early in the 19th century. The original packhorse route to Chatsworth left the village via Pig Lane, where the pigsties can still be seen, and it was replaced by the 'New Road' to the west of the village, making Beeley one of the first villages in the land to receive the benefits of a bypass.

The Duke's Barn was built in 1791 and housed the carthorses and drays which provided transport for both farm and estate. Today it houses a school for the deaf. For many years the old horses, their usefulness at an end, could be seen being quietly led down by the church and across the road into the Horse Pasture, where they were shot and buried. The sad little mounds can still be seen down by the river.

Beeley Old Hall, still a ruggedly beautiful old house and situated at the north-eastern end of the village, was the manor house until 1559, when it was replaced by 'The Greaves', subsequently renamed 'Hill Top' by the Savile family in 1667.

An interesting experience is to visit Hob Hurst's House, the Bronze Age tumulus up on Beeley Moor, especially at dusk. This ancient tomb is said to hold supernatural powers and if you listen carefully you may hear the voices of the original inhabitants.

⌘ BELPER

Belper is an old market town, and was originally known as Beaurepaire. It is in a pleasant valley of the river Derwent, and the scenery around the town is of more than usual interest with railway, road, river and canal all running parallel.

Before the Industrial Revolution Belper was already famous as a centre of nail-makers. The nailers were a rough lot of people in the 18th century, and they worked in the nail shops, one of which still stands in Joseph Street in the area known as 'The Clusters'.

One of the buildings that dominates the Derwent valley on the main Derby to Matlock road is what is known as 'The Belper Mill', founded by Richard Arkwright and Jedediah Strutt in 1776. The workers employed in the cotton mill

River Derwent and East Mill

in the beginning were mostly children, whose nimble fingers could tie threads together which had broken on the machines, and they could crawl behind them to keep them clean. Most of the mill workers were housed in Long Row which stands to this day just as it did when it was built in 1792–93.

In the 1900s out-workers were employed to embroider men's socks up the sides, called 'chevining'. This process was usually done by the light of a paraffin lamp or candlelight by mothers at home at night whilst the children were tucked up in bed. The hosiery industry made a great impact on the community, employing many in the early days making lisle, then pure silk stockings and then later, nylon tights.

The River Dove at the foot of Biggin Dale

⌘ BIGGIN

Lying midway between Ashbourne and Buxton, just off the A515, Biggin was first mentioned in 1223. Then called Newbiggin, it consisted of a grange with several small farms, owned by Garendon Abbey and farmed by monks of the Cistercian order.

The church, dedicated to St Thomas, was consecrated in 1848 and built of limestone acquired from a nearby field on The Liffs road. On the Sunday nearest to 12th September the annual Wakes was kept, with special church services, and on the Monday, led by a band and carrying a banner, the Loyal Order of Ancient Shepherds would parade the village, ending at the Waterloo inn for the traditional roast beef and plum pudding. Another custom was the locking-out of the teachers. On Shrove Tuesday, the older boys would arrive at school early and tie the doors. When the teachers arrived, the children would chant: 'Pancake Day is a jolly day, If you don't give us a holiday, We'll all run away'. The teachers would then pretend to be angry, but when the doors were opened, prayers said and register taken, the school would close for the day.

The Newhaven House Hotel was the last public house in England to have a perpetual licence. King George IV was so impressed by the warmth and hospitality of the then landlord, when he stayed there on his journey north, that he granted the licence, which applied until a few years ago when it closed for repair.

⌘ BOLEHILL

Bolehill lies on the slope of Barrel Edge to the north-east of the town of Wirksworth. It derives its name from the 'bole', or smelting hearth, which was situated on the hillside above the village.

In the 17th century the village consisted of a few miners' cottages situated close to the Bage Mine, with only tracks and a packhorse way connecting it to nearby towns and villages. The opening of the Nottingham to Newhaven turnpike in the following century improved communications although the route through the village was changed within a few years of the opening, probably due to land slippage. This is still a problem today, with Stoney Hill/Kernal Hill being closed to vehicles since 1969 despite several attempts to repair it.

When lead mining was at its peak the miners' holiday was a great event. For a week in May, country dancing took place on the green, there was a gingerbread stall, donkeys to ride and greasy pole to climb – with a prize at the top of – a leg of mutton.

As the lead industry declined the people of the village sought employment in the quarries, the mills and on the railways, and the growth of employment brought new people to the area.

The Bage Mine was explored in 1980 by the Wirksworth Mines Research

Looking across the Derwent Valley, from Riber to Bolehill

Group. They found a very wet, but beautiful, shaft showing yellows, blues and greens in its lower reaches. The group descended to a depth of 376 ft. One of the members, John Jones of Kegworth, found two specimens of Cromfordite, a very rare mineral formed from translucent green crystals. Its name derives from the place where it was first discovered.

⌘ BOLSOVER

'Honour and principle did not seem to be known in the place, and we soon found that drunkenness and unchastity were no crimes, except in the clergy' – so wrote Mrs Hamilton Gray, the vicar's wife in 1829, referring to Bolsover. Let's hope this is no longer a fair description as Bolsover's famous 17th century castle, built by the Cavendish family, is visited by thousands of people each year.

In the main road is a public house called the Hudson Bay. Canada is a long way from Bolsover you may think, but this pub was originally built as a house for his mother by Peter Fidler, a local lad who worked for the Hudson Bay Company in

Bolsover village

the 18th century as a surveyor. A Peter Fidler Society still exists in Canada.

Standing in front of the Hudson Bay, and looking down into the valley, can be seen the evidence of years of coal-mining. Not all of it is pit heads and spoil heaps, as it includes a magnificent village built by craftsmen for the miners.

Behind Sherwood Lodge is evidence of an Iron Age entrenchment which would have encircled the settlement. This leads to an open space known today as Kitchin Croft, named after John Kitchin, a clay pipe maker of 1739. Pieces of clay pipe are still found and are known as fairy pipes, legend being that they were used by fairies under the earth.

The White Swan doubled as a moot court from the Middle Ages until the early 19th century. Bolsover received its charter from Henry III in 1225, and the original grid pattern of streets is still discernible.

⌘ BRACKENFIELD

Brackenfield was known as Brackenthwaite in medieval times. The green is the centrepiece of the village (the second largest green in Derbyshire after Killamarsh).

The village green used to have a stream and many wells, which have been filled in, but in 1986 the villagers decided to start a well dressing event, in order to raise

Ogston Reservoir in the Amber Valley

funds for the church. Every year since, on Spring Bank Holiday weekend there is a celebration which centres on the old school (parish hall) on the north side of the green.

Brackenfield has a picturesque reservoir, which is overlooked by Ogston Hall. The reservoir was constructed 1955–1960 in the valley where several houses and Ogston mill once stood. The old Trinity chapel is now a ruin, hidden on the wooded hillside. Trinity chapel was featured on all the county maps from the 16th century onwards, and was built on the site of the original medieval chapel, mentioned in the Domesday survey (1086).

One infamous character from Brackenfield's past is Samuel Mather. Some say he was a local sheep thief in the early 18th century, who was hanged for his crimes at the crossroads on Tansley common. Another version is that he committed suicide in an old barn, not far from Brackenfield green. He took his own life because of the unhappiness caused by an illegitimate daughter. He lies buried at a road junction beneath a date stone, which is to be found set in a wall in the part of the village now known as Mathersgrave.

⌘ BRADWELL

The village name is probably derived from 'Broadwall', possibly referring to 'Grey Ditch', a broad fortification to the north of the village used by settlers to resist attack from the Brough side. In his fascinating book *Bradwell Ancient and Modern* published in 1912, local author Seth Evans captures the essence of the village – 'Its steep winding streets, if streets they can be called – and all sorts of queer little out of the way places running in and out in all directions, break-neck, skew-tilted, beginning everywhere, leading nowhere …' aptly describes the village.

Like so much of the Peak District of Derbyshire, the village of Bradwell owes much of its prosperity and architecture to the firm economic foundation provided by the 18th and 19th century boom in the lead mining industry.

But it was not only the lead extraction and associated smelting operations on which the village, tucked beneath Bradwell Moor, depended in years gone by. The weaving of both silk and cotton was commonplace within its cottages and Bradwell later became known as a centre of milliners and hatters, with no less than seven hatters in business at one time.

One of the village's most famous inhabitants was Mr Samuel Fox, who invented the folding umbrella, and who also founded the Stocksbridge steelworks. Born the son of a shuttle maker in 1815, in a cottage in Water Lane, he became something of a local benefactor, donating £100 towards the building of the parish church. He also presented a site for the vicarage and bequeathed a trust fund to be distributed amongst the poor annually.

⌘ BRAILSFORD

The name Brailsford is derived from 'a burial ground by the ford'. In the Domesday Book the village is listed as having a priest, half a church, 24 villagers, three smallholders and a mill. The reference to the church describes its position between Brailsford and Ednaston, shared by the communities. The church is thus in the fields away from the traffic, a delightful setting.

The people are down-to-earth, with an innate sense of the fitness of things and an appreciation of a quirky streak. Thus a diligent farmer, much plagued by a lazy and feckless neighbour whose fences were always in disrepair, found a way of dealing with the problem. Cows which strayed were milked before being returned;

horses did a morning's ploughing and the ram served a flock of sheep. The point was made, no words were needed – the fences were mended.

On the borders of Hulland Ward and Mercaston, on a lane between Cross-O-The-Hands and Brailsford, is the tiny place of worship called Halter Devil Chapel. The chapel was built in 1723 on to the end of the farmhouse and buildings by Francis Brown, who reformed after years of drunkenness. One dark night he attempted to halter his horse and mistakenly caught a cow which he thought was the devil. Hence the name Halter Devil Chapel.

John Yates, a bachelor, lived at Brailsford North, in the early years of the 20th century. He was a breeder of the shire horse, and his first stallion was called *Agrivator*, the sire of his finest horse which he called *Brailsford All We Want*. The descendants of John Yates still breed shire horses to this day.

⌘ BREASTON

Breaston is mentioned in the Domesday survey as a small collection of thatched cottages made of timber, wattle and daub. This manor was given by William the Conqueror to Richard de Busli, one of his loyal followers. As was common practice, the land, unfenced and unhedged as we know it now, was farmed in strips by families. Clear traces of these strips can still be seen on Breaston Park.

At the time of Domesday there was no church in Breaston, the people having to walk across the fields to St Chad's at Wilne, or All Saints at Sawley, to worship. The beginnings of the parish church of St Michael appear in records around the year 1200. The priest would come from Sawley or Wilne to say mass in the new little church, but for many years all baptisms, weddings and funerals took place at Wilne. There was no burial ground at Breaston and until 1824 coffins were carried on shoulders across the fields to Wilne. The 'Coffin Walk' is still a public footpath over the fields from Breaston to Wilne. As with all churches, many changes have been made to St Michael's over the centuries, resulting in today's mellow, grey stone building; make sure that if you visit, you ask to see the 'Breaston Boy'; legend has it that, during the building of the church, a little boy would come and sit, chin in hands, watching the men at work, and that the 'Breaston Boy' is the mason's humorous portrayal of him.

The bed of the now defunct Derby Canal can still be followed behind the houses on the north side of Longmoor Lane, and at the Navigation inn a large basin which enabled barges to be turned round is clearly visible.

⌘ BURBAGE

The name means a mountain stream or the valley of a stream and if you stand on the hills around the village, you realise how well it is named, as you see the little stream coming from Axe Edge and meandering through the fields below.

View towards Buxton from Grinlow, near Burbage

In the 17th century, Burbage was an agricultural area, then, later came the era of quarrying, lime burning and lead and coal mining; it is thought that stone was quarried here by the Romans, since there are remains of a Roman road, and a burial ground, Poole's Cavern, was found under Grinlow Tower (known locally as Solomon's Temple). The first lime workers lived in little houses made in the hillocks of ashes left from the lime burning.

The quarry workers showed great interest in the Methodist church and in 1858 built a chapel in Ladmanlow, but when the Duke of Devonshire gave the land for a church to be built in Burbage, the Methodists took their chapel down – stone by stone – and rebuilt it, almost across from the church.

⌘ BUXTON

Although no longer classified as a village, Buxton, of course, started off as one and owes its development to its natural springs with their constant temperature of 28°C and the curative powers of their nitrogen and carbon gases. Mention Buxton Water today and most people think of the bottled variety but it is because of the thermal springs and their healing properties that Buxton has its place as one of the oldest and most fashionable spas in the country.

During the Roman occupation of Britain, Buxton was an important station en route from Manchester to Lincoln, and it is probably due to the Romans that the baths developed, only to fall into neglect on the departure of the legions. Buxton's fame revived, however, and around 1600 the Earl of Shrewsbury built the Hall to accommodate visitors. Four times between 1573 and 1582 Mary Queen of Scots, in the charge of the Earl of Shrewsbury and his wife, Bess of Hardwick, was taken to Buxton to find relief from chronic rheumatism and neuralgia. In 1596 Queen Elizabeth I ordered her travels so that for three weeks she was near enough to Buxton so that her favourite, the Earl of Leicester, could have its water brought to him daily.

The influence of the Devonshire family, who inherited the Buxton estates by descent from Bess of Hardwick, is everywhere in evidence, and it was the fifth Duke who was responsible for the Crescent, built in 1780 and rivalling the one in

Buxton Pavilion Gardens

Bath. The Devonshire Royal Hospital too is magnificent, said to have the widest unsupported dome in the world. The Pavilion and Pavilion Gardens are well worth a visit and the recently restored Opera House has world wide renown.

Lover's Leap in Ashwood Dale is a huge natural cleft in the limestone rocks and was so named because two runaway lovers on a horse leapt the chasm to avoid pursuit. The geology of the area is particularly interesting and there are collections of the local Ashford marble and the unique Blue John stone in the museum.

⌘ CARSINGTON & HOPTON

Carsington and Hopton are two old mining villages which lie between the market towns of Wirksworth and Ashbourne. In the 7th century, a monk named Betti came down from Northumberland and set up a preaching cross, which now stands on the village green.

The church of St Margaret is of 12th century origin but was rebuilt in 1648 and stands on the bottom slopes of Carsington Pastures. An entry in the register dated 29th September 1668 reads: 'Sarah Tissington died. Born without hands or arms. She learned to knit, dig in the garden and do other things with her feet.'

Carsington reservoir at sunset

Carsington Pastures is about 365 acres of open grazing land which rises steeply above the village to a height of over 1,000 ft above sea level. On the summit there is a large stone landmark, marked on the Ordnance Survey as the King's Chair, but known locally as the Lady Chair. The ground is scarred with remains of lead mines, the main source of wealth for the village for several hundred years and worked first by the Romans, who also brought with them the pretty blue and yellow pansy, known as heartsease.

For many years no building of any kind took place in Carsington but, in the last two decades of the 20th century, a bypass was built and the new Carsington reservoir was constructed by the Severn Trent Water Authority.

The main road originally ran in front of Hopton Hall until a later road was built. That is the reason for the 16th century Miners Arms inn standing with its back to the main road, facing the little lane which was the old road.

Hopton Hall gardens are enclosed by a high brick wall built by Sir Philip Gell, who founded the almshouses in Hopton in 1719. The wall is hollow with a stove at one end. The hollow wall conducted heat from the fire around the wall, against which were grown various kinds of fruit trees. This warmth, together with its south-facing position, ensured an early crop of peaches and other fruits for the house.

⌘ CASTLE GRESLEY

Castle Gresley is a village situated in rural countryside on the A444 in South Derbyshire. Its history begins with the Gresley family. A parcel of land was handed down to two sons, one parcel of land contained the church and so became Church Gresley, the other contained a wooden castle that was built on a well-known local landmark, Castle Knob. The castle was built between 1086–1090. Nothing remains of it today, but this plot of land became known as Castle Gresley.

Every village has its ghosts and Castle Gresley is no exception. When fog or mist hangs in the air a lady dressed in white might be seen in a wooded area known as the Nursery. There is a reservoir in the Nursery supplied by a spring, and many years ago a lady was drowned there – hence the name White Lady Springs. The reservoir was owned by the brewery and supplied the brewery with water; later it became a fertilizer factory, then a pickle factory, a mill, a tape-factory and then Toons Carpets, and this is where a second apparition appears as an old lady who visits the upper rooms.

Since early in the 19th century, the village has relied heavily on its coal, but in the 1940s and 1950s it suffered from subsidence. Houses were propped up, cracks appeared in the roads, while the spoil heap at the Gresley Colliery poured poisonous gases into the atmosphere. The other colliery in the village was Cadley Hill. Both these collieries have now closed, Gresley in 1967 and Cadley Hill in 1988. The subsidence and the spoil heaps have now gone and in their place is pleasant countryside.

⌘ CASTLETON

Castleton lies at the head of the beautiful Hope valley, encircled by hills and overlooked by Mam Tor – the 'shivering mountain' – with the remains of a Celtic hill fort on its summit. The village derives its name from the castle built by William Peveril, bastard son of William the Conqueror.

The village is unique for several reasons. There is the locally-mined semi-precious stone known as Blue John, which is found nowhere else in the world and

The path to the Peak Cavern

which in former times was used for making large ornaments still to be found in many stately homes today. Nowadays it is mainly used for small pieces of jewellery which are on sale in the local gift shops.

The Garland ceremony is also unique to Castleton. It takes place on 29th May every year and is a survival of the ancient 'Green Man' fertility rite. It was suppressed during the Commonwealth years but revived in 1660 to celebrate the restoration of King Charles II, and has continued ever since. The 'King', wearing a large, beehive-shaped garland of flowers covering his head and shoulders, rides on horseback through the village with his 'Consort', followed by the village band, and young girls in flower-bedecked white dresses dancing to the Garland tune. After the First World War, maypole dancing was introduced and at the conclusion of the ceremony the 'Queen' (the top-most posy of the garland) is placed by the 'King' on the village war memorial.

Visitors have always come to Castleton, attracted by the beautiful hill scenery and grand walking country, and the four deep underground caverns with their fasinating geology. Queen Victoria and Lord Byron were two notables amongst the many visitors of the past.

⌘ CHAPEL-EN-LE-FRITH

Chapel-en-le-Frith is known as the 'Capital of the Peaks', and lies just off the A6 road between Buxton and Stockport.

After the Norman Conquest, and possibly before, the area was part of the Royal hunting forest of the High Peak, and within the parish of Hope; this meant almost a day's journey to attend a funeral or a marriage. The foresters and keepers petitioned for a chapel of ease, which was granted and the first church was built in 1225. It became known as the Chapel in the Forest. Later it was dedicated to the martyred Thomas à Becket, and for 700 years the successors of the foresters preserved the right to elect their vicar.

Chapel-en-le-Frith's largest and most widely known employer is Ferodo Ltd, producers of friction materials for the motor industry. The company was formed in 1897 by a local gentleman, Mr Herbert Frood, who had observed the problems of local carters on the steep hills of the Peak District. He patented a brake block made from woven cloth impregnated with resin, the first of its kind in the world, and from this small beginning sprang the whole range of friction materials that we know today.

The local beacon of Eccles Pike is situated to the south-west and rises to a height of 1,250 ft above sea level. Many people find it an invigorating walk to the summit which, when reached, gives wonderful views of the surrounding countryside. Each Good Friday, local churches form a procession of witness and a cross is carried to the top and placed there.

Church Brow, Chapel-en-le-Frith

⌘ CHARLESWORTH

Charlesworth is a pretty village nestling on the side of the Pennines. It lies on the borders of three shires, Lancashire, Yorkshire and Cheshire but is part of Derbyshire.

Long Lane runs from the centre of the village to the 'Top Chapel' (Charlesworth Congregational chapel). Here during a violent storm, a traveller found refuge on his way over the Coombs and Monks Road. He vowed to build a 'house of prayer' in thankfulness for his deliverance. The actual date of the building of the first chapel is uncertain but there is a reference to this as far back as 1291.

The Catholic church stands in lovely surroundings on the edge of the river Etherow, the boundary between Broadbottom and Charlesworth. This church was built in the year 1895 for the many Irish immigrants who came over to this country after the potato famine, settling in Broadbottom and working in the mills in the area.

When Rev Goodwin Purcell arrived in 1846, he found no church, no vicarage and no school. All three were realised by his hard work and efforts. He walked to Lands End and raised £1,500 and also collected money from wealthy individuals and the parishioners, to reach his target of £2,700. In 1849, the church of St John was opened and he turned his attention to a school and vicarage. This he was pleased to see opened in April 1851. In five years he had achieved his ambition and by 1873, 1,000 churchgoers attended.

⌘ CHINLEY & BUXWORTH

With the coming of the Peak Forest Canal and Tramway at Buxworth in 1806 and the railway through Chinley in 1867, the two villages were no longer isolated areas with a few scattered farmsteads. Then, after 1806, Buxworth grew and rapidly achieved fame as an inland lime port, despatching 70 narrow boats each week loaded with coal, limestone and powdered lime, stone and slates.

The nucleus of Chinley began when Mr James Waterhouse of Plarr Farm (now Heatherlea) built 20 cottages and a shop in 1852 at Chinley End. In 1862 he built the first Methodist church in the centre of Chinley, known as 'The Preaching Room'.

After the widening of the railway line the new large Chinley station was built in 1902, a junction for Manchester, Liverpool, London and Sheffield. This railway venture involved the building of two joining curved viaducts. The station had five waiting rooms with big fireplaces, a refreshment room and a bookstall. A stationmaster (Ould Sammy Hart the locals called him) in top hat and frock coat, with a huge timetable in his hand, rushed up and down the six platforms, sending trains 'all over t'country'. Something like 100 trains a day passed through Chinley station with 180 on August Bank Holiday.

Until his death in 1951 at 83 years of age, Mr Joseph Waterhouse of Albany House (built by saving all his threepenny bits over many years) chronicled the happenings of the village church and all his family in verse. He had a very dry sense of humour and his verses were witty and humorous. Some he would write in broad Derbyshire, then later bring up to date in King's English. He was a notable preacher and sometimes flautist and organist.

⌘ CHURCH BROUGHTON

Church Broughton lies close to the south-west boundary of Derbyshire. Because two of the large farms in the village were part of the Duke of Devonshire's estate until early in the 20th century, there had never been a resident lord of the manor. Apart from the church, built by the monks of Tutbury in 1300, with its little steeple atop a tower, there is also a timbered house and plenty of cottages from the 17th and 18th centuries. The name Broughton means the farm by the brook. However, because the brook was never large enough for a mill, the village's prosperity depended on agriculture.

In the 19th century, the village was one of the largest in the area. There was a busy brickworks, a wheelwright, blacksmith, four shoemakers, three butchers, a bakery and other small shops. The inhabitants, however, were so unruly that the Duke had one of the first police houses in the county built in 1855 (now called Peel

House, in Church Road). A cell for men opened into the hall, while that for women was above, by the bedrooms.

In 1864 William Auden, uncle of the poet, came to Church Broughton as vicar. He was followed by another nephew Alfred, who organised the closure of the Royal Oak public house in 1917.

⌘ CRICH

Approached from any direction it is apparent how appropriate is the pre-Roman name of Crich, meaning hill. Geologically it is an anticline, being a mass of limestone rising to 955 ft above sea level, pushed up through the surrounding

The Tramway Museum at Crich

millstone grit. Lead was mined here from Roman times and the limestone quarried for lime burning and road making. An 18th century painting of Crich shows lime kilns in the centre of the village in the field known as Kiln Crofts.

The parish church of St Mary is the most important building, dating from 1135 with a Norman nave, columns and font. Another fine building is the Baptist chapel on the Market Place, and of great interest is the Wesleyan chapel built in 1765 and the oldest still in use in the country. John Wesley came here to preach in 1766 when the chapel stood on the edge of common land. Behind the chapel rises the gritstone edge of the Tors.

Crich Stand, the fourth monument on the site since 1760 offers a spectacular view. It was built in 1923 as a monument to the men of the Sherwood Foresters who died in the First World War. It stands out as a landmark for miles around and its lantern shines after dark. On the first Sunday in July a pilgrimage is made to the Stand by men of the Sherwood Foresters & Worcester Regiment with their mascot, standards and regimental band.

In days gone by Crich boasted many trades – a saddler, milliner, scythestick maker, candle maker, shoemakers, six tailors, blacksmiths, wheelwrights, joiners, also two surgeons, a druggist, a solicitor and three academics, not to mention nine public houses.

Today, it continues to thrive. Quarrying continues at a great rate with modern machinery. The stone now goes to maintain the motorways, conveyed by huge lorries. The old worked-out area of the quarry is now the home of the National Tramway Society which preserves and restores these beautiful vehicles.

⌘ CROMFORD

Sir Richard Arkwright, the cradle of the Industrial Revolution, 'satanic mills' – are words synonymous with Cromford, but there was habitation here long before Arkwright came, it being mentioned in the Domesday Book as an outlier of the manor of Wirksworth. The original hamlet nestled beside the 'crooked' ford crossing the river Derwent – hence its name Cruneford, to Crumford then Cromford.

The bridge now spanning the river is unique, as the upstream side has rounded arches and the downstream side three pointed 15th century arches.

With the arrival of Richard Arkwright in 1771 and the building of his three cotton mills, the need for housing for his workers led to the building of the village on its present site, nestling at the foot of the surrounding hills. North Street is a fine example of workers' houses, considered models for their period.

The Market Place is dominated by the Greyhound Hotel built by Arkwright. Here the Manchester stage coach stopped for stabling and victuals. Impressive Rock House – Arkwright's home – gave him a view over his mills. Gracious Willersley Castle standing above the Derwent, started by Sir Richard but burned

Cromford from Black Rock with Derwent Gorge beyond

down before it was finished and not completed until after his death, is now the headquarters of the Methodist Holiday Guild. During the Second World War it served as a maternity hospital for mothers from the East End of London, and there are many who can proudly say they were born in a castle.

⌘ CURBAR

Overlooking the main part of the village of Curbar there is a ridge of hills which stretch for a couple of miles. It is always fascinating to watch people climbing the steep rocks.

From the bottom of the hill the Bar Road climbs up through the village. From the top of the hill, you can see that it was a Roman road and there is a straight road across the moor over a mile long.

Just over 30 years before the plague in Eyam, Curbar suffered in a similar way. On the moors there are the gravestones of the Cundy family, who lived at Grislowfield Farm, Curbar. A man by the name of Sheldon is also buried up there. There are also a number of tombs just below the Wesleyan Reform chapel

Early morning mist from Curbar Edge

which are dated 1632. It would appear that Curbar suffered before Eyam.

Near the moor there is a small square house with a round roof; originally this was used to house prisoners who were being taken across country. It is now a private house.

Cliffe College in Curbar is used for the training of those who wish to join the church as ministers or as special workers. At the end of the 19th century it was used to train missionaries but they were moved to London for training.

⌘ DALE

Not the most accessible of places, Depedale, or Dale Abbey as it is now called, has close ties with its neighbouring village of Stanley, and what it lacks in size it makes up for in history. Here one can find the great east window of the ancient abbey, and a tiny church just 26 ft long by 25 ft wide, said to have the largest chalice in use in England – being nine inches high and 15 inches round.

The church shares the same roof as a farmhouse which was rebuilt on the same site in 1883. The building was used as an infirmary for the abbey and later a pub known as the Blue Bell. They owe their origin to a Derby baker named Cornelius who, between 1130 and 1140, had a vision to go to Depedale and live a life of meditation and solitude.

On the south side of the valley Cornelius cut a hermitage, measuring six yards by three yards, in the sandstone cliff. Well-preserved, the cave has a doorway and two windows. He discovered water nearby – said to have healing qualities.

The abbey was completed in the early 13th century and the magnificent window arch, 40 ft high and 16 ft wide, still stands as a reminder of this important and wealthy settlement.

All Saints' church was a 'Peculiar', which meant that it did not come under the authority of the Bishop and prior to the 1754 Marriage Act couples could marry without banns being read.

The Cat and Fiddle, thought to be Derbyshire's only surviving post mill, stands on the site of an earlier mill. It provided a landmark for miles around and was workable until 1987 when the 18th century mill lost its sails in a gale.

The river Dove below the village of Doveridge

⌘ DOVERIDGE

The Domesday Book tells that Doveridge boasted, amongst other things, a parish church and a water mill. Dropping down from the church, a footpath passes the site of the old water mill, demolished in the 1970s. Approaching St Cuthbert's by the main path you enter a 'tunnel' of branches formed by an ancient yew tree, reputed to be some 1,200 years of age. According to legend, Robin Hood was betrothed to his lady under its boughs. In recent times these boughs have been propped up with timber and restrained by chains to prevent them blocking the way.

The village primary school is today housed in a modern building but in the 18th century the few lucky children who received education were taught in dame schools which were held in various houses throughout the village, notably 'The Gables' in Lower Street, a fine old house which has been carefully restored. In 1797 the first purpose-built village school was completed, paid for with money from bequests by two village ladies, Mary Burgh and Lucy Bakewell. This building is still standing and is used as a private dwelling.

Heading from the centre of the village towards the church one arrives at a crossroads on which stands Doveridge Well. The village has several wells but this one is of most importance, being a handsome focal point. The well is now capped over and a garden surrounding it is maintained throughout the year by members of the Doveridge Women's Institute, who also supplied a seat which was installed there in 1951 to mark Festival of Britain Year.

⌘ DRAYCOTT & WILNE

In order to get their Derbyshire lead from Derby to the river Trent at Trent Lock, the Romans built a straight road between the two. A small community developed along it about six miles from Derby. It was mentioned in the Domesday Book in 1086 as Draicott or Dry Cote. About a mile to the south by the river Derwent there was a settlement which we now call Wilne, the original name meaning 'a clearing in the willows' which sounds a wet and marshy place. A church was recorded there in AD 822 dedicated to St Chad, the Bishop of Lichfield whose diocese covered the area. The Domesday Book also records a manor and a mill; the latter has survived in various forms through the ages, and at present it is the maker of fireworks and military pyrotechnics.

The folk at Wilne gradually moved to Dry Cote as this was higher and drier, not subject to flooding and eventually they merged.

For centuries this was a farming community, but as industry grew so did Draycott. Coal was mined in the more northern area of the county, and transported in carts drawn by donkeys as far down as the river or the canal. Draycott folk are traditionally called 'Neddies'. The reason was that the market place was the changing point for the coal-cart donkeys.

The landmark in Draycott is the large Victoria mill, its clock-tower visible from miles around. This mill really brought industry to the village. Its size was the same as Noah's Ark; 300 cubits long, 50 cubits wide and 30 cubits high. When it was completed in 1907 (having been badly damaged by fire in 1902) it was the largest manufacturing mill in Europe.

⌘ DRONFIELD

Dronfield is thought to mean the open land where there are drones (male bees). It is situated in the north-east of Derbyshire halfway between the city of Sheffield to the north and Chesterfield to the south. It is bordered on the west by open countryside which adjoins the Peak District National Park – a mere three miles away.

Many of the old buildings are in the High Street and Church Street area. One of Dronfield's more unusual and interesting buildings stands near the top of the High Street and is the Peel Monument. Built of gritstone in 1854, it is a tribute to Sir Robert Peel, and celebrates the repeal of the Corn Laws in 1846. It is a much photographed and sketched feature in Dronfield.

In 1662 Dronfield was granted a market by Charles II, but in the 18th century, due to the nearness of Sheffield and Chesterfield, the market went into decline and ceased to exist. It was revived on a nearby site in 1980, and is thriving today.

Close to the Monument on High Street, is a house known as 'The Cottage', dating from the 16th century. It is believed to have been owned by Lord Byron (1788–1824), though there is no proof of this.

It is said that a smell of thyme may always be noticed near a footpath leading from Dronfield to Stubley. There is a legend that tells of a young man who murdered his sweetheart there when she was carrying a bunch of thyme.

⌘ DUFFIELD

Duffield is on the A6 five miles north of Derby. Duffield in Appletree was mentioned in the Domesday Book of 1086, being one of the five Wapentakes or Hundreds listed under the County of Derby.

The railway runs through the village and Duffield station was once known as a 'Top Hat' station as several of the railway hierarchy lived here. A row of houses was built specially for railwaymen who were transferred to Derby from the North. Nowadays Duffield station is a 'halt' and one can board a little train and take a very pleasant journey to Matlock.

Duffield endowed school has been in existence since the 1600s and there is now also the Meadows primary school and Ecclesbourne school. There was formerly a girls' school: the headmistress, Miss Dorothy Benner, was a figure of great authority, her cane always lying on top of her desk which was on a platform. This lady, carrying a lot of weight, used to make the floor shake when she dropped off her stool to point to the blackboard. Another colourful character of the 1920s and 1930s was Mrs Laura Butler of Tamworth Street, who used to light the gas lamps in the village each evening in winter.

Duffield Cricket Club have played cricket on Eyes Meadow for over 100 years. There are football, rugby and hockey pitches as well. The Duffield Carnival, organised by the Community Association, is also held annually on Eyes Meadow.

There are churches of several denominations in the village. There is the 12th/ 14th century parish church of St Alkmund; Trinity Methodist church; the Baptist church; St Margaret Clitherow Roman Catholic church; and the Emmanuel community church.

⌘ EARL STERNDALE

Earl Sterndale, five miles south of Buxton, lies 1,100 ft above sea level in the Peak National Park. It is ringed by beautiful hills such as Parkhouse, Chrome and High Wheeldon. Chrome is recorded as being the highest hill in the county, and High Wheeldon was given to the National Trust as a memorial to the men of Derbyshire and Staffordshire regiments who gave their lives in two World Wars.

The first recorded mention of Earl Sterndale is in 1244, when it was known as Stenredile. This may reflect the nature of the terrain in those days – a stony and sterile dale.

The church of St Michael, Earl Sterndale

The church of St Michael was built in 1828 and it has a Saxon font. This font was shattered when the church was virtually destroyed by incendiary bombs on the night of 9th January 1941, the only one in the Derbyshire Diocese to be damaged by enemy action. The font was repaired, the church rebuilt, and rededicated in July 1952. Wakes is held on the Sunday nearest to 11th October. Tradition has it that the man who is most drunk on the Friday before the Wakes is elected Mayor for the year.

The Quiet Woman inn is reputed to be over 400 years old. This unusual name, one of only three in the country, is said to derive from the too talkative wife of a landlord who was decapitated in consequence! It has the sign of a headless woman and the quotation 'Soft words turneth away wrath'.

Woodbine Cottage was once the home of Billy Budd, who fought in the Afghan War in 1880, and who marched from Kabul to Kandahar, a distance of 350 miles, wearing no boots but his feet wrapped in cloths. He is buried in the churchyard.

⌘ ECKINGTON

Eckington, which is in north-east Derbyshire, is seven miles north of Chesterfield. The name Eckington is of Saxon origin, meaning the township of Ecca.

In medieval times it was a small but important settlement, which was later engulfed by development when coal deposits were extensively worked throughout the area. It is a long sprawling village, with typical picture postcard scenes of its manor houses and cottages built of the local Derbyshire stone.

The parish church of St Peter and St Paul dates from the year 1100 and is of exceptional architectural interest, still retaining the original Norman doorway. In a field at the back of the church, near the river Moss stands the Priest's Well where the parish priest used to draw water for the needs of the church.

Sir Reresby and Lady Sitwell live at Renishaw Hall, which is surrounded by parkland and a golf course on the outskirts of Eckington. The Hall has been the home of the Sitwell family for nearly 400 years and has become famous through the writing of Edith, Osbert and Sacheverell Sitwell, father of the present owner. A novel feature at the hall is the vineyard begun in 1972.

A market is held each Friday on Market Street, adding life and colour to the centre of the village. The Civic Centre, also on Market Street, is widely used for many different functions and activities, and stands beside the swimming pool and library.

There are many pathways for people to enjoy to the surrounding villages and through the wooded valley of the river Moss, a tributary of the Rother. This area, now rich in wildlife, was once a centre of industry, relics of which can still be seen today.

Grindsbrook Clough on the Pennine Way

⌘ EDALE

The valley is deep, 1,250 ft in the middle, so that the sun sets early and frosts are keen. The five small communities or booths that formed the old centres of life are strung out in a line along the south facing side, upslope from what was once the marshy, wooded, wolf and fugitive-concealing valley floor. Two newer groups of houses lie near the station and a mill on the river Noe and a small number of isolated farms and barns are dotted among the fields. Just a few private houses line the road.

If Edale has a centre, it is the middle booth, Grindsbrook, where trees conceal the church, school, post office and houses. Nearly all are made of stone and the wide fields are contained within stone walls which stretch up the valley sides until the land becomes too steep to improve and fields give way to open sheep pastures or bracken and heather moor and eventually, on the northern rim, to crags of millstone grit which edge the Kinder Plateau.

The past scene is of a few families visited only by jaggers (packhorse men) who plied their trade, cheese and salt from Cheshire or woollen bales from Yorkshire, along a narrow track from Hayfield, through the booths to cross the rushing brook at Grindsbrook by the way of a lofty stone packhorse bridge and on out of the valley up Jaggers' Clough and Crookstone to Derwent.

New blood arrived when the old corn mill became a cotton mill, and an even greater influx came when the railway was built. The population rose from 335 in 1881 to 960 in 1891 and a shanty town grew up near Barber Booth where the one and a half mile long Cowburn tunnel was excavated in 1888.

⌘ EDENSOR & PILSLEY

Edensor and Pilsley, and the hamlets of Calton Lees and Dunsa, all lie on the Chatsworth estate. Many of the inhabitants work at Chatsworth House, the home of the Duke of Devonshire.

The Saxon village of Ednesoure, now Edensor (pronounced Enzor) is a small model village surrounded by a wall. St Peter's church dominates the village, and was built on the site of the old church in 1870. A patronal festival is held on 29th June and people from Pilsley, Calton Lees and Dunsa join in a weekend of celebrations. Many Americans come to see the grave of Kathleen Kennedy in the ducal burial ground. She was killed in an aircrash after her husband, Lord Hartington, the present Duke's brother, was killed in the Second World War. President Kennedy came to see his sister's grave in 1963 on a visit shrouded in great secrecy for security reasons. The only casualties of the day were the churchwarden's hens, which were swept up with the presidential helicopter and never seen again!

Edensor and Pilsley both lie within the Chatsworth Estate

Sir Joseph Paxton is also buried in the churchyard. He had long associations with Chatsworth and, among many other achievements, designed the Crystal Palace.

To preserve the 'model village' appearance, no vegetable gardens or pig sties were in evidence, allotments were provided up the village and washing had to be hung in the drying ground, again out of sight. Now everyone takes a great pride in their gardens, which are a delight to see, and what they do with their washing is their own affair!

⌘ ELVASTON

Elvaston is a large rural parish east of Derby and uneasily sharing a boundary with the city. The parish encompasses the hamlets of Elvaston, Thulston and Ambaston (originally Ealvoldstune, Torulfestune and Eanbaldstune), ancient settlements named after their respective chiefs. This area has been populated for at least 3,000 years and farming was so well established by 1086 that there was 'land for 17 ploughs', calculated as about 500 acres, a quarter of the present parish area.

In the time of Henry VIII the local manor with its lands came to the Stanhopes, who lived in the castle. The local authority bought the castle, its surrounding

Elvaston Castle

parkland and the Home Farm and in 1969 this was opened as a Country Park, one of the first in the country, now identified by English Heritage as a 'Park of Special Interest, Grade 2'. At the top of the avenue from the A6 there is a fine pair of iron gates, painted in blue and gold and known locally as the 'Golden Gates', which are reputed to have been taken from Madrid by Napoleon and acquired by the Earl of Harrington, possibly as 'spoils of war'.

The parish church, dedicated to St Bartholomew, is close to the castle and dates back to the 12th century, with additions and alterations in the 14th century, and contains some fine monuments and carved screens.

⌘ ETWALL

A photograph taken from St Helen's church tower a hundred years ago shows little change from the view today – the curving road with its large old houses, the top pub, the rectory, the almshouses and beyond that the open country.

Etwall is mentioned in the Domesday Book as Etewelle, and was originally named after the Saxon king Eata, whose well or spring lies below St Helen's church; Etwall still has the remains of nearly 70 wells.

The almshouses, rebuilt 300 years ago round an open courtyard close by St Helen's church, are perhaps the most outstanding feature of the village. They now provide ten attractive and much sought after homes for retired 'locals', married or single. Quite a change from the days when a fence was erected and a warden appointed to lock the men in at night and throw any women out! The final transformation to the almshouses was the addition of the famous Robert Bakewell gates which had for some years languished in a school cellar. What now proudly welcome visitors to the almshouses, had for over 200 years and flanked by two lodges, guarded the entrance to Etwall Hall.

The site of the Hall with its lake and grounds became the site of the John Port school. Dilapidated after war-time occupation by the forces, its home-farm land sterile, it appealed to the Director of Education as a suitable place for setting up two new schools, a grammar and a secondary modern in the centre of the village. Later these became the focus of the present John Port comprehensive school which now has in the region of 2,000 students travelling from a wide radius. The name of the Port family who bought land and married into local gentry, has been associated with Etwall since the 15th century.

⌘ EYAM

Eyam (pronounced 'Eam' as in 'steam'), is situated in the Peak District, five miles north of Bakewell, and derives its name from the Anglo-Saxon 'Ey' meaning water and 'Ham', a settlement. The permeable millstone grit sandstone in the hills to the north of the village above Eyam shales, is impervious to water and ensures that rain

The Riley graves of the Hancock family, Eyam

water issues out from the shale as a series of springs down the one mile length of the village street. In 1588, twelve sets of stone troughs were built along the village street and the spring water was conducted to the troughs by pipes; thus Eyam became one of the first villages in the country to have a public water system.

Eyam is famous as the Plague Village. A widow, Mary Cooper, and her two sons lived near the church in what is now called Plague Cottage. Lodging with them was a tailor named George Viccars. It is said that cloth he had ordered from London, where plague was raging, arrived damp and was spread out to dry. This released plague-infected fleas. Within days Viccars fell ill and died. He was buried on 7th September 1665. Fifteen days later fear spread when young Edward Cooper died, quickly followed by several neighbours.

William Mompesson, the rector, supported by Thomas Stanley, a former incumbent, fearing the infection would spread widely, asked the villagers to quarantine themselves from the outside world. They arranged for food and medical supplies to be left at agreed points on the village boundary, eg Mompesson's Well and the Boundary Stone. The church was closed and services were held in Cucklet Delf, a valley nearby, where the Plague Commemoration Service is still held annually. There were no funerals and families buried their own dead near their homes, as at Riley, where Mrs Hancock buried her husband and six children in eight days. The plague ended in October 1666. In 14 months it had claimed 259 lives out of a population believed to have been about 350.

⌘ FENNY BENTLEY

Life in Fenny Bentley has for a long time revolved around the school, the church and the pub. The old school building is now leased to a scout group who use it as an outdoor activity centre; the new FitzHerbert School was opened in 1970.

The beautifully proportioned church of St Edmund has a dominant position in the village. An annual summer fete organised by the church and school jointly is still eagerly anticipated by villagers.

The Coach and Horses dates from the 16th century, and as the name implies, it was formerly a coaching inn.

Perhaps the most imposing building along the main road is Cherry Orchard Farm. This dates from the 15th century, and at one time had twin towers and battlements. It was the seat of the Beresford family. Sir Thomas Beresford fought at Agincourt, and is buried in the church. His wife, Lady Agnes, had 21 children, and everyone with the surname of Beresford is said to be descended from them. In fact there is an annual convention in the village, when Beresfords come from all over the country, and indeed from abroad, to reunite.

Until recent years, the village was mainly built along the main road. The Bentley brook follows the road, and in the days before the widespread knowledge of public health, it was a convenient form of sanitation for those living in cottages facing the road!

⌘ FOOLOW

Foolow is a small, picturesque limestone village situated in the Peak National Park, two miles west of Eyam, in whose parish it is. The name is said to mean multi-coloured hill or burial ground and is first mentioned as Fowlowe in 1269.

Since Roman times it has been a lead mining area and although this ceased some years ago, remains of the activities of 'the old man' can be seen today with mine shafts and spoil heaps still visible. Many of the waste heaps have now been removed for the fluorspar, which was in lead mining days, considered useless.

Much of the village dates from the 18th and 19th centuries, and as with many villages within the Peak National Park, new building is not allowed to extend outside the village bounds. The manor house is a fine example of a gentleman's residence and was built in the 17th century. Overlooking the village green is the Old Hall which has been two residences for many years.

The pond and green, with its cross (dating from the Middle Ages) and bullring, remain the focal point of the village. The cross bears the date 1868 on its plinth. This is the date it was removed from the site where the chapel gates now stand and

The picturesque limestone village of Foolow

it was placed in its present position. The church, which is dedicated to St Hugh, was built in 1888 and in 1928 the porch was erected with stone from the disused smithy across the road from it.

When the village was a farming community, the green was always muddy and indented with hoof marks. Today, many of the farm buildings are dwellings, the grass is regularly mown, spring bulbs flourish and visitors picnic and watch the ducks swimming on the pond.

⌘ FROGGATT

Froggatt is a small village with some 200 inhabitants; above it to the east is Froggatt Edge where many well-known climbers have gained experience. To the west the river Derwent winds through the woods and across it stands an interesting 18th century bridge, wide enough for single file traffic only but with inlets over the piers for pedestrians to step aside. The bridge is unusual in that it has a large central arch nearer the village side and on the farther side a smaller arch, the latter probably part of the original bridge which spanned the much narrower stream existing before the Derwent was dammed at Calver. In the 1930s land on the far side of the bridge used to attract visitors to the water's edge and was nicknamed Froggatt Lido.

Froggatt was so-named not because of the presence of frogs but because there were originally 17 freshwater springs in the village. At least three can still be seen, one near the bridge, one along Hollowgate and a third called 'Top Spout' halfway up the green.

The village was once owned by the Duke of Rutand who, in the 18th century, had 17 stone cottages built by local stonemasons. There are still a few cottages in their original state, several listed buildings, but many have been modernised and others enlarged.

A highlight of village life is the Annual Horticultural Show. Originally there was a 'Cow Club' but in the 1930s a Mr Carnall, Ernest Fletcher, John Morton Senior and Mr Hattersley met in Riley's Cowshed and Froggatt Show was born.

⌘ GLAPWELL

Glapwell is a small village situated on the A617 Mansfield to Chesterfield road, approximately two miles east of Junction 29 of the M1, just inside the Derbyshire border with Nottinghamshire.

In the Domesday survey, the hamlet of 'Glapewelle' is listed with Bolsover, and by the 13th century it was owned by the de Glapwell family, one of whose heirs married into the family of Woolhouse, who resided at Glapwell Hall in the 17th century. The Hall, which was allowed to fall into disrepair in the early years of the

The unusual Froggatt Bridge

20th century, was demolished in the 1960s. The remains of the conservatory, the stables and a small building thought to have been the coachman's cottage, still stand on the site, and in very dry weather, the foundations and carriage drive can clearly be seen on what is now the village football pitch.

In the 1880s, the Sheepbridge Coal and Iron company sank the first shaft of what was to become Glapwell Colliery, and together with the coming of the railway, this resulted in an increase in the population of the village. It is said that the colliery was sunk on its site because the Hallowes family, who lived at Glapwell Hall at that time, refused the company permission to sink where they originally wanted because they did not want to have the outlook from the Hall spoiled by pit chimneys, smoke and pitheads! The colliery finally ceased production in 1974.

⌘ GREAT HUCKLOW

Great Hucklow is a former lead mining village, which although small – only 100 or so inhabitants – has always been a very active one. It now has a thriving Women's Institute and a group called 'Community Spirit' formed a few years ago by the youngsters, mainly teenagers, who arrange social events and a Well Dressing during August.

In 1927, Great Hucklow had its very own theatre company, created by Dr L. Du Garde Peach, a local author/playwright, whose father was the local minister. He set about forming a company called 'The Village Players' from residents in and around Great Hucklow. They were allowed use of the Holiday Home in the early days – a place where children from deprived areas were brought during the summer months for holidays arranged by the Unitarian chapel. During the winter months the plays were staged there and were planned to coincide with the full moon, so that players and audience would have a 'guiding light' to and from performances – for most had to walk!

Their first production was *The Merchant of Venice*, and this proved so successful that many more classics were staged over the 40 years they were performing. Many more in fact were also written by Dr Peach himself, and acted in the Derbyshire dialect. So successful were the players that it was decided perhaps they should have their own theatre. An old Cupola barn at the other end of the village was purchased for £200 – and the land adjoining it for £100. People came from miles around to this small village theatre and in the early days used to bring their own refreshments and even cushions to sit on, and rugs for warmth. Unfortunately when its creator died, so did the theatre. The building is now used as a Scout centre for visiting groups.

⌘ GREAT & LITTLE LONGSTONE

In the Domesday Book, Langes Dune or Tune is recorded as the name and means Long Settlement. One can possibly assume that Longstone Edge, which is now called Longstone Moor, was the long settlement to which this refers.

The most famous inhabitant of Longstone must be G. T. Wright Esq, of the Wright family of the village. He compiled the 'Longstone Records', which is the authoritative document of both Great and Little Longstone.

More recent characters included Jack Holmes, a small man of vast joviality, forever happy, singing and continually whistling. Always neatly dressed in knee breeches and leggings, one could, as the saying goes 'set one's watch by him'. He always appeared at certain points in the village at certain times each and every day. Another was a relation of his, Bill Holmes. Bill was mine host of the Crispin inn in the days of the horses and traps. But his main fame was in poultry shows, for he excelled in breeding Black Leghorns. At one of the poultry shows held in the Longroom at the old Bull's Head, which is now the Monsal Head Hotel, Bill decided that the legs on the birds he was showing were not black enough, so the black lead pot came out, and the hens' legs were well and truly blacked. Well, you can guess the outcome when the judge held the birds by the legs.

Little Longstone near Monsal Head

⌘ GRINDLEFORD

Grindleford – a strange name you may think, but a long way back in time grindstones were fashioned from the local stone at quarries in the area and carried across the ford of the river Derwent. The setting of the village is absolutely beautiful; surrounded by hills with the wooded Padley Gorge and the river Derwent running through its centre.

In the area known as Upper Padley is Padley Chapel, the only remaining part of Padley Hall, and the wide mouth of Totley railway tunnel. Exactly 300 years separates important happenings at these places and first of all we go back in time to the year of the Spanish Armada, 1588.

The Fitzherberts who lived at Padley Hall were staunch Roman Catholics, with priests under their roof in order to conduct the Mass. The then owner, Sir Thomas, was in prison in the Tower of London, and through domestic treachery, on the 12th July 1588, a raid took place during which Sir Thomas' brother John and two priests, namely Nicholas Garlick and Robert Ludlam, were arrested and taken to Derby Gaol. On 23rd July, the two priests were tried, found guilty of high treason and condemned to death by hanging, drawing and quartering. Sir John was also found guilty but allowed to live by paying £10,000 and living out his life in the Fleet Prison. Today Roman Catholics make a pilgrimage every year to the restored chapel on the Sunday nearest to 12th July in memory of the two priests, who are known as the Padley Martyrs.

Moving ahead 300 years, the building of the Totley railway tunnel began in September 1888. It runs from Totley in Sheffield to Grindleford and is the gateway to the Peak District by rail. It is a remarkable feat of engineering, being three miles 950 yards long and was completed in 1893.

⌘ HATHERSAGE

Situated in the Peak National Park at the entrance to the Hope valley, Hathersage is the first village on the A625 after leaving Sheffield and marks the division between the Dark and White Peaks. There is some controversy about the origin of the name Hathersage but anyone looking up from the village to the surrounding moorlands in late summer will understand why it is commonly believed to be a corruption of 'Heather's edge'.

The village boasts seven old houses or 'Halls' said to have been built by a member of the Eyre family during the Middle Ages for seven sons. People who have lived there claim that at least three of these – Highlow, Northlees and Moorseats, are haunted. Northlees and Moorseats are also well known for their association with Charlotte Brontë who wrote her novel *Jane Eyre* after a visit to her former school friend Ellen Nussey, the sister of the vicar of Hathersage. She used the two Halls as models for the homes of Mr Rochester and St John Rivers.

Abandoned millstones on Millstone Edge, near Hathersage

The shop where Jane Eyre tried to barter her gloves for a 'cake of bread' is said to be modelled on a building in the village, and the Brontë link is carried further in that the landlord of the George Hotel at the time of Charlotte's visit was called Morton – the name she gave to the village where Jane sought help.

Traditionally Hathersage was the home of Robin Hood's companion Little John; his grave is in a prominent position in the churchyard.

⌘ HATTON

Hatton is an ancient village extending one and a half miles close to the busy A50, west of Derby. Travelling south we enter the village at the Salt Box junction. Many years ago this area was thought to be an important stop on the 'Salt Run', carrying salt from one end of the country to the other. It is referred to as the Turnpike and serves as an oasis to many truck drivers who find refreshment at the Salt Box Cafe, which won an award of 25,000 tea bags in 1989 for the 'Best Cafe Cuppa'.

Many of the inhabitants commute to nearby towns and cities but others are employed by very successful local industry. The most notable is the Nestle factory, which draws much of its work force locally. The factory was built in 1901 in a dairy farming area where the essential ingredient, milk, was available for the production of sweetened condensed milk.

The Nestle's 'Bull', a steam whistle, was used at the onset of the Second World War as an air raid siren for the district until the more familiar 'Wailing Winnie' was installed and later transferred to the local fire station. Since 1959 the factory has concentrated solely on producing various blends of instant and ground coffee, the delicious aroma of which wafts all over the village.

Just beyond the railway line is a fine stone bridge over the river Dove, linking Hatton and Tutbury. In 1831 workmen removing gravel from the Dove found silver coins, and working upstream they discovered a hoard of coins of various currencies; apparently a scramble commenced and people flocked to the area with their spades. The treasure of over 100,000 coins was said to belong to the Duchy of Lancaster, but only 1,500 coins were forwarded to officials.

⌘ HAYFIELD

Hayfield, with a population of 3,000, is an ancient village nestling at the foot of Kinder Scout. The church, St Matthew's, dates back to 1386 with the present church having been rebuilt in 1818 on top of the first church.

Hayfield was the venue for two cattle and sheep fairs each year, one held on 12th May and the second on 10th October. Shepherds met at the Pack Horse inn on the

River Kinder behind 'The Bear Pits', Hayfield

12th July each year and one shilling was paid for each lost sheep returned to its owner. After a lapse of several years the Sheep Dog Trials and Country Show was revived and is held at Spray House Farm, Little Hayfield in September.

The village was very popular at Easter and Whitsuntide when train and bus loads of hikers and ramblers came in their hundreds to walk over the moors to Edale and to the Downfall. Sadly, the railway station closed in January 1970. There was a Mass Trespass of the moors in 1932 which was organised by keen ramblers to enable them to retain their freedom to walk over Kinder Scout, and a plaque was erected in the quarry at Bowden Bridge, Kinder, to celebrate the 50th anniversary in 1982.

Hayfield has some very old pubs. Whilst the Royal is not the oldest, it certainly has a history. It was built as a parsonage in 1755 for Rev J. Badley. He died in 1765. His wife discovered that the deeds had been made out in her husband's name, so she sold it and it became the Shoulder of Mutton. Restored as a vicarage in 1805, there was controversy over the new incumbent. He was turned out of the vicarage and the building became the present Royal Hotel.

⌘ HEAGE

Heage or High Edge is described in Woolley's *History of Derbyshire* as 'lying scattered all about'. The village is in two main parts, Heage itself and Nether Heage (formerly High Heage and Low Heage). Neither village has a centre and consists of houses and cottages scattered along the roads and lanes, with some small estates of modern housing. The name is from the Anglo-Saxon 'Heegge' meaning high, lofty or sublime.

Situated in the Amber valley area, the main occupation of the original inhabitants would have been farming. There are still many family-owned farms today, rearing sheep and dairy cattle and growing cereal and root crops. In the early days of the Industrial Revolution coal mining and the ironworks at Morley Park and later at Butterley were major employers. There was a drift mine in the village (now a small housing estate) and coal was mined at nearby Hartshay and taken on horse-drawn barges along the Cromford Canal. Village folk also gained employment at the cotton mills and hosiery factory in Belper.

The oldest building in the village is probably Heage Hall, situated in Nether Heage, which is now a farm. Parts of the Hall date back to the 15th century. Later occupants of the Hall were the Shore family, who also owned and worked Heage windmill and water mill (no longer in existence) at the bottom of Dungeley Hill. The windmill has six sails and is a landmark seen from miles around, especially from the west.

The parish church, dedicated to St Luke, was originally built of wood, but was destroyed by a violent tempest in June 1545. Rebuilt in 1661 and enlarged in 1836, it has no square tower or spire, but an unusual octagonal bell tower on the north side of a barn-shaped structure, with the oldest part of the church at right angles to this.

⌘ HIGHAM & SHIRLAND

Although Higham and Shirland form one parish, they are two villages, both situated on the A61 Derby to Chesterfield road. Higham branches off from the A61 and its main street follows the line of the old Roman Rykneld Street.

The parish was in existence by the time of the Norman Conquest and by 1220 the foundations of Shirland church had been laid. This imposing gritstone building was refurbished to make room for the poor parishioners; the old box pews had only room for the gentry.

The famous industrialist John Smedley built a Wesleyan chapel in Higham. He thought it too far for his workers to travel to Shirland in bad weather and so arranged for them to worship nearer home. Later he also built a school for 70 children.

The cross at Higham was repaired in 1755 at a cost of three shillings and sixpence but the steps are still the original. The whole cross was moved to a safer position when road traffic became heavier.

Higham Farm Hotel houses in its foyer one of the three wells left in Higham. At one time there were as many as 23. Bull Farm used to be the Black Bull inn and legend has it that the infamous highwayman Dick Turpin once stayed there. In 1864 a coal mine was dug in Shirland, and by the end of the century the colliery employed 500 men and improvements in their working conditions led to amenities for the village in the form of a bowling green and a Miners Welfare. The site of its spoil heap is now a golf course and little evidence is left of the old mine workings.

⌘ HILTON

Hilton is situated on the A516 Derby to Uttoxeter road, eight miles from Derby and five miles from Burton-on-Trent.

The Wesleyan Methodist chapel situated in Main Street was built in 1841 and is still a thriving place of worship. A Primitive Methodist chapel (now a private residential cottage) was erected at a later date and is still known as 'Tell Me Why' by those who recall the words shown on a window facing the road.

On entering Hilton from Derby, you pass the Old Talbot public house, a 16th century cruck building. The oldest building in Main Street is Wakelyn Hall, built in a style that places it among the principal houses of the county in the 15th century. It is reputed once to have been an inn and to have hosted Mary Queen of Scots on her journey to imprisonment in Tutbury Castle. Whilst being restored in the 20th century, a font, almost certainly Saxon, was discovered below a pump. This is thought to have come from the chapel of ease which existed in Hilton during the 13th century, and during the 1500s was dedicated to Sir John Port of Etwall.

At one time there was a smithy which was part of the King's Head public house. A large gritstone boulder used to stand on the corner and an old seafaring man of the village used to sit making ships in full rig, out of a fowl's breast bone.

The old Hilton gravel workings are now owned by the Derbyshire Naturalists Trust and are a bird sanctuary and nature reserve.

⌘ HOLYMOORSIDE

Some say 'Holy', some say 'Holly', and some just say 'Moorside', but they all refer to Holymoorside, a village about three and a half miles to the south-west of Chesterfield. 'Holy' is supposed to refer to the fact that in the Middle Ages, monks from Beauchief Abbey near Sheffield were sent via Holymoorside to Harewood Grange, a tiny hamlet on the moors nearby. But as these were the erring members of the fraternity, and Harewood Grange was a monastic 'house of correction', they would hardly have acquired a reputation for holiness.

It is more likely the name is derived from an Anglo-Saxon word meaning 'hill-clearing'. It is quite easy to see the reason for 'Moorside'; even today the purple expanses of Beeley Moor and Eastmoor are only a few minutes' drive away and, before some of the area was enclosed during the 18th century, the heathery slopes came right down to the centre of the village.

Today most people earn their living outside the village, travelling daily to Chesterfield, Sheffield or even further afield. A hundred years ago things were very different. Self-sufficiency was the motto and there were tradesmen and craftsmen of all kinds in the community. Farmers were predominant, but there were also miners, quarrymen, lead miners and smelters, blacksmiths, butchers, grocers, joiners, basket-makers and besom-makers, even a taxidermist!

There are some evocative names in the village. Water comes from the 'Whispering Well', Wellspring House is close by, and Pennywell Drive reminds us of the days when piped water was not the norm. There is Cornmill Cottage, Laundry Yard, Cathole and the Pinfold, but Sewerage Lane is hardly an inspired choice! Hipper Hall, a 16th century farmhouse with an even older tithe barn, is probably the oldest building in the village.

⌘ ILKESTON

Ilkeston, the Queen of the Erewash Valley, stands proudly atop a substantial hill. Mentioned in the Domesday Book, Ilkeston was originally an Anglo-Saxon community as is borne out by parts of the ancient church of St Mary.

Ilkeston has seen many differing trades and industry, the manufacturing of lace being one of those still in existence.

For all its industry, Ilkeston is a very green place as is most evident if you should climb the 99 steps of the tower of St Mary's and look around. Trees and greenery abound and the parks and flower beds are a credit to the community. It enjoys one of the finest cricket grounds in the county with wide views of the surrounding countryside, presented to the people many years ago by the Duke of Rutland, who at one time owned a great deal of the land here.

Every October most of the streets in the centre of Ilkeston are closed to allow the Annual Charter Fair to come into being. Created over 700 years ago the Ilkeston Fair is now perhaps one of the largest street fairs in the country and is well worth a visit.

Ilkeston might well at one time have become a spa, for about 100 years ago a natural spring produced waters beneficial to certain ailments. The Bath House was a haven of relief to many in the late Victorian age. However, sadly the

The Market Place and St Mary's church, Ilkeston

properties in the water were not maintained and the spring dried up. The main street is known as Bath Street and is the only reminder of what might have been.

⌘ IRETON WOOD & IDRIDGEHAY

Idridgehay lies in the beautiful valley of the Ecclesbourne river which rises near Wirksworth and has its confluence with the Derwent in Duffield, and one mile south of Idridgehay lies Ireton Wood. Idridgehay is the larger of the two villages. The oldest house, a thatched timber-framed building now called South Sitch was built in 1621 by George Mellor, whose initials with those of his wife are still to be seen in the fabric. Much later the then owner of South Sitch, Robert Cresswell, was a principal benefactor with James Milnes of Alton Manor when the church of St James was built in 1855.

The railway came to Idridgehay in 1867, built by the London Midland who were intent on having their own line to Manchester. With this in mind, although it was and still is a single track, all the bridges were built double width. In the event another route was found, but it became a very busy branch line carrying commuting passengers and milk from local farmers who converged on the station from far and wide every evening at 5 pm. Although the line is occasionally used to carry stone from the Wirksworth quarries the station was closed some years ago and is now a private house. The local pub, the Black Swan, is an attractive old building which according to a plaque at the entrance was used by George Eliot as the original for 'The Waggon Overthrown' in her novel *Adam Bede*.

⌘ KILLAMARSH

Killamarsh is in the north-east corner of the county on the border with South Yorkshire. It was mentioned in the Domesday Book as Chinewoldmaresc, which is believed to originate from Chinewold's marsh – Chinewold being the lord of the manor. It was a scattered agricultural community, but coal has been mined here for more than 500 years.

With the building of the Chesterfield Canal, which passed through the centre of the village, and the railways, Killamarsh became an important trading place. From the 19th century, coal mining was the most important industry. There were several coal mines in the vicinity and when boys left school they automatically followed their fathers into mining. In his book *Colliers and I*, F. J. Metcalfe, a former rector of Killamarsh, tells of his affection for the colliers and his efforts to keep young boys from bad influences and to stop them from swearing.

In St Giles' church is a rare stained glass window depicting the crowned Madonna and child. This escaped the ravages of Cromwell's Puritans. An interesting item on the outside wall of the church is a stone tablet which records the fact that John Wright, a pauper, died in 1797 in his 103rd year. The Methodist church too has a beautiful stained glass window which shows a miner at work. The Congregational church in High Street is known as 'The Church on the Hill' and the Ebenezer gospel hall is sometimes called 'The Church in the Field'.

Rother Valley Country Park, which caters for all kinds of water sports, is partly in Killamarsh. National competitions are sometimes held here. There is also a lake for fishing and a nature reserve where many species of birds are to be found.

⌘ LONGFORD

Longford lies at the centre of a triangle joining the towns of Ashbourne, Derby and Uttoxeter. It consists of scattered homes and farms and lies along an old Roman road, Long Lane, which joined the camps of Derby and Rocester.

At one end of the village is St Chad's church, set amongst magnificent lime trees, Longford Hall, cottages and farm buildings. Sir Nicholas de Longford settled here in the 12th century and the church was built at this time. It still has its Norman arches with extensions added in the 15th century. There are effigies in the church of three de Longfords in their Crusaders' armour and the last of the de Longfords and his lady in 16th century costume. As you leave the public road to the right you can just see what remains of the almhouses.

Longford Hall is set in delightful grounds

The original Hall was rebuilt in the 16th century and extended 200 years later. In 1942 a fire caused serious damage and it lost its top floor, but was otherwise restored. The Cokes, related to the Earls of Leicester, took over the estate after the de Longfords, and they owned it until the beginning of the 20th century.

A mill was built along the road in the 11th century and there is still one there which is used as a private home, but this was built in 1837 by Arkwright. It was in working order until 1956 but the machinery has now been handed over to the Arkwright Society in Cromford.

Opposite the mill is the first cheese factory built in England in 1870 by a Dutch-American named Cornelius Schermerhorn, with local support, including Lord Vernon and the Coke family. It is a wooden structure and is boarded outside and plastered inside with an open space between for the circulation of air. The factory was a co-operative and produced 20 cheeses a day and butter, but it was eventually overcome by competition from imported cheeses and larger factories.

⌘ MARSTON MONTGOMERY

Marston Montgomery takes its name from the Montgomery family who owned the lands of both Marston and the neighbouring village of Cubley at the time of the Domesday Book, and this distinguished it from Marston-on-Dove, only a dozen miles away.

The small village lies off the main road and so is lucky to avoid through traffic. Many houses have attractive views across pastureland towards the Weaver hills in Staffordshire. It is a pleasant spot, particularly in the spring when the damson blossom is out, making a froth of white all along the narrow lanes.

The church of St Giles is said to have the oldest ecclesiastical masonry in Derbyshire, with a Norman font and Saxon and Norman arches, but much of it was rebuilt in the 19th century. It has a low sloping roof and a bellcote, and nestles into its surroundings with some old tombs and an ancient yew.

Perhaps the most notable architecture in the village itself is the manor house, an impressive black and white 17th century house with a massive external chimney stack. There is also a fine Georgian-fronted house in the village, the rear part being a century older. But probably the oldest house is in the attached hamlet of Waldley. This is a farmhouse with the date of 1632 engraved in the timber, though parts are believed to date from 1512. In fact, the village is surrounded entirely by dairy farms, several with interesting 17th century houses.

In 1987 the Derbyshire tradition of well-dressing was revived in Marston Montgomery, after a lapse of 49 years. This was done to celebrate the 50th anniversary of the erection of the village hall, called the Coronation Hall as it was put up in King George VI's Coronation year.

A dressed well showing an aerial view of Marston Montgomery

⌘ MATLOCK

The Domesday Book recorded old Matlock as 'Meslach', one of six hamlets forming part of the large manor of Metesford, named after Matlock's original ford. Meslach became Matlac, Matloc and finally Matlock, meaning 'an oak where was held the local moot or parliament'.

During the Second World War a German plane, thought to be lightening its load to aid its escape over the hills, peppered this area with tracer bullets and shells. RAF planes often screech through here now, their pilots practising flying through the valley, sometimes so low that from high ground, it is even possible to look down on them.

It is a steep climb up Bank Road and Rutland Street and sadly there are no longer any trams to take the strain. Cable-hauled, and the steepest tramway on a

Matlock from above the Derwent at High Tor Grounds

public highway anywhere in the world, trams ran for 34 years, until 1927. The tramway was built when the railway, together with plentiful spring water, had brought prosperity, fine shops, new homes and fresh employment to the area. More than 20 hydros operated at the turn of the 20th century. Local mill owner John Smedley spearheaded the growth of hydrotherapy in Matlock. His 'mild water cure' used all manner of showers, bathing contraptions, bandages and towels, together with copious amounts of spring water at varying temperatures. 'Nay, it's not to drink – ay, tha's reet now – tha sits int Sitz bath'. His own purpose-built palace was the hydro, famous nationally and internationally, visitors coming to 'take the cure', or simply to be cosseted in his opulent surroundings. Noel Coward and novelist John Wyndham came. Dame Clara, mother of Ivor Novello, lived there. At afternoon tea in the Winter Garden, Violet Carson played the piano.

⌘ MATLOCK BATH

Matlock Bath's distinctive name is due to the discovery of thermal water, which led to the formation of baths. These springs contain lime and salt solutions. Over many years the solution hardened to form beautiful open-work forms of rock. Spread over the ground for a third of a mile, beds from one ft to 20 ft deep became known as tufa, or to locals as marl. Objects left in the water were 'petrified' or turned to stone. The rock was quarried and sold all over the world for rock gardens. When the road known as Temple Walk was cut, the antlers of a moose were found embedded in the rock and they were sent to the British Museum.

In 1696 a Bath was formed in the tufa, the waters being thought beneficial not only to drink but also in which to bathe. This led to the first commercial bath being built in 1698 and was the main reason for people visiting the locality. The Wishing Well built from tufa can still be seen, with its date '1696' above, within the Temple Road car park. The water is piped under the car park and reappears to tumble over the rocks into a pool. For generations youngsters with jam jars tied with string have fished for tadpoles and minnows in its warm water.

The white edifice on the Heights of Abraham overlooking the valley has enticed visitors for over a century to wend their way up the steep wooded hillside to venture into the depths of the Masson and Rutland Caverns (lead mines once worked by the Romans) and still fascinating the curious. Today visitors are whisked through the air by cable car from the banks of the river Derwent to the Victoria Tower.

The heyday of Matlock Bath came with the advent of the railway in 1849, when it brought thousands of visitors to the town. Today people have their own transport and although the line is still open, the station built in the style of a Swiss chalet is now a wildlife centre.

⌘ MELBOURNE & KING'S NEWTON

Situated in the south of the county, eight miles from Derby, Melbourne contains within its parish boundaries the picturesque village of King's Newton. Having around 4,000 inhabitants, Melbourne is known today chiefly for its market gardening and the manufacture of shoes, but in the Middle Ages it was a place of some considerable importance, to which the size of the church and castle bore witness.

The church of St Michael with St Mary, believed to be on the site of an earlier Anglo-Saxon building, is acknowledged to be one of the finest examples of Norman architecture to be found in a parish church, and visitors are curious to know why such a magnificent building should be found in a relatively small Derbyshire village. The fact is that in the middle of the 12th century, when the church was built, the river Trent formed the boundary between the civilised south of the country and the more barbaric north.

One man who has had a lasting influence was born in Quick Close, Melbourne. In 1841 a temperance meeting was to be held in Loughborough and he arranged for the Midland Railway to run an excursion train, carrying 570 people from Leicester

The village of Melbourne

and back for one shilling per person. From this he began to arrange excursions for pleasure, taking a percentage of the sale of the railway tickets. And so began a world-wide travel business: the man's name – Thomas Cook.

Like Melbourne, King's Newton has Saxon origins. Its principal building is the Hall, built in 1910. Across the road from the Hall stands the Hardinge Arms, and it was from here that one William Taylor sold his home-brewed ale to the local people. Finding an apple seedling growing in the thatch of his roof, he decided it was worth removing carefully and growing in his garden. It proved to be a winner and, increasing his stock by budding and grafting, he introduced the 'Newton Wonder' to the horticultural world.

⌘ MILLERS DALE

Millers Dale is a hamlet in the parish of Tideswell. It stands on the left-hand bank of the river Wye, two miles from Tideswell and eight from Buxton, sharing its name with the dale in which it lies.

During medieval times two corn mills were built, the river powering their machinery. Ancient upland trackways, which converged in the dale, gave the mills their names. The Wormhill mill, probably the older of the two, stood in the upper reach of the Wye, with the Tideswell mill lower down.

The river Wye at Millers Dale

In recent times the flour mill has undergone some alteration and change of use, to a craft supply centre, with world-wide connections. Some time ago the derelict Tideswell mill was demolished, making a site for a pumping station feeding the Chapel-en-le-Frith area. Stone from the original walls was used to house the bore-hole and its machinery. The 150 year old water wheel was restored and placed adjacent to the pumping station. Stone walls enclose the whole site.

Richness of flora and fauna along the dale sides has resulted in the area being designated a Site of Special Scientific Interest. The reserve, which is managed by the Derbyshire Wildlife Trust, is part of a disused limestone quarry.

⌘ NORBURY & ROSTON

Norbury and Roston are closely knit villages in the parish of Norbury.

Norbury appears in the Domesday Book as Norberie or Nordberie, the northern defence on the Dove (while Sudbury was to the south). Today Norbury is a scattered community and visitors may be surprised to find the church, dedicated to St Mary and St Barlok, tucked away out of sight with only two houses to keep it company. The 14th century chancel, with stained glass windows that predate the Black Death, is dominated by the great east window. This was restored over a period of ten years in the 1970s.

The 17th century manor house beside the church was the home of the Fitzherbert family for 700 years, and the stone building at right angles to the church is all that remains of the Norman house. The National Trust now owns the manor, and the stone hall may be seen by appointment.

Anyone familiar with the works of George Eliot will know that Norbury is Adam Bede country. He was born on Roston common in the house bearing his name, and Bartle Massey's school, where he went, is the original village school on Green Lane, once the old turnpike road.

Roston, spelt Roschintun in the Domesday Book, centres on the area known as the Bullring. Whether this was once associated with bull baiting or the cattle market, which was held in Shields Lane is unclear. There are two disused Methodist chapels in the village. The story goes that there was once disagreement as to where a chapel should be built and the building materials would disappear from one site to be found on the other in the course of the night. No agreement being reached, two chapels were built a few hundred yards apart.

⌘ NORTH WINGFIELD

North Wingfield was originally a farming community with some small scale coal and iron-stone mining. It grew to its present size to accommodate the development of large collieries in the area. The Great Central Railway opened a new line in 1892–93 to serve these collieries and provide means of transporting coal to London. The miners were generally brought in from outside the village and were housed in colliery company terraced rows. These houses have now disappeared and the mines worked out, with the population travelling to more distant places of work.

North Wingfield has many old and interesting buildings, including its village church where the roof still has much of its original 14th century tracery beamwork. The 80 ft high tower, some 500 years old, boasts an even older great bell, and in the recesses of the chancel lie knights in chain armour believed to be from the 13th century and of the local Deincourt family.

The old Elizabethan rectory house was greatly extended in 1690 and contrary to most Elizabethan buildings has the middle arm of the letter 'E' missing. A plaque on the front wall of the old rectory bears the inscription 'Nunno deficiente plus ultra' which roughly translated means that the cash ran out before the extension could be built.

The closing of the pits and the withdrawing of the railway service left a large amount of derelict land. This has been reclaimed by the County Council and the Five Pits Trail created giving miles of traffic-free pathways for walking, cycling and horse-riding with picnic sites and magnificent views across the Derbyshire countryside. Woodlands, ponds, and meadows have been created making the Trail a haven for wildlife.

⌘ OCKBROOK

Ockbrook is two villages in one. There is the old settlement which Occa, an Anglo-Saxon, established along the banks of the brook around the 6th century and from which the village derived its name. Alongside it is the Moravian settlement, one of only three in the country, which sprang up in the second half of the 18th century.

The church of All Saints became the parish church around 1600. Before this it was a chapelry of Elvaston. It has two notable features, one being the tower which was built in the 12th century, to which the prominent broach spire was added sometime later, and secondly the Norman font which was not appreciated by the Victorians and thrown out into the garden of the former rectory for many years. This was restored to its rightful position in 1963.

Following the arrival of the Moravians there was a great change in the village. Large houses were built and the community increasingly attracted the middle class and more affluent members of society. Work also diversified. There were four silk glove makers, four shoemakers and someone who made straw bonnets. The Cross Keys inn, where stockings were made for Queen Victoria and her court, still has its knitters window.

The jewel in Ockbrook, viewed on its hilltop site from the west as travellers pass along the A52, is a terrace of red brick Georgian buildings, the Moravian

Settlement. From here one has a magnificent view across the village and the valleys of the Trent and Soar to the hills of Charnwood Forest.

⌘ OSMASTON

Osmaston at the time of the Domesday survey was called Osmundestune. The original name of the parish was Whitestone.

The picturesque village pond stands at the bottom end of the village and is overlooked by the two oldest thatched houses in the village. At the back of these are two new houses, the first to be built in the village for many years.

The old St Martin's church was built in the 15th century to replace an earlier building of wickerwork. In 1843 the foundation stone was laid for another church. This opened for divine service in June 1845 and was also dedicated to St Martin.

Osmaston, and the seat made from horseshoes

The village hall was opened on Coronation Day 1937 to replace the old Victory Hut. The hall has a thatched roof and is used for various functions. The school use the kitchen every day for the preparation of meals, and the children dine there. Opposite the village hall are four thatched cottages which are known as Coronation Cottages.

Outside the Shoulder of Mutton public house there was a weighbridge, used to weigh stone which was being used to build Osmaston Manor.

Leading into Osmaston Park used to be an avenue of lime trees, but these were destroyed in February 1962 by a gale. The avenue led down to Osmaston Manor, which was built in 1849 and demolished in 1964 when Sir Ian Walker and family moved to Okeover Hall near Ashbourne and took the Okeover name. The smoke tower from the manor still stands today.

The polo field which once belonged to the manor now belongs to the village and is used by football clubs, weekend caravan clubs and the annual Ashbourne Shire Horse Show which in August 1990 celebrated its centenary.

⌘ OVER HADDON

The village of Over Haddon is situated two miles south-west of Bakewell, in the Peak District. It clings to the sides of a steep valley, and overlooks the beautiful Lathkill Dale. Lathkill Dale became a National Nature Reserve in 1972, and was the first to be so designated in Derbyshire by the Nature Conservancy Council (now English Nature).

Mandale Mine is one of the earliest recorded mines in Derbyshire, and is mentioned in the 'Quo Warrento' of 1288, because it was producing and selling a lot of cheap lead. By 1615 some of the Mandale workings were 300 ft deep. Many of the miners' paths up the daleside to Youlgreave are still in existence, one even having paving stones which, although covered in grass, can still be made out.

Although the lead was running out, the Mandale aqueduct was constructed in 1840 to carry water from the reservoir to work the waterwheel. However, in spite of this modernisation, these workings were short-lived, and the machinery was sold in 1852. The remains of the aqueduct can still be seen, however, in the form of its stone pillars.

The story of mining in Over Haddon must make mention of the extraordinary events of 1854. In one of the lead mines on Manor Farm gold was found in some lava. The owners had it investigated, and it was found that although gold did indeed exist it was deep down, and in such small quantities that no profit could be made. However, a company was formed, gold was extracted and sold for £25 per ton. It generated so much excitement that hundreds of people rushed to invest in the mine; discussions even took place to build a railway connecting Over Haddon and Bakewell to transport the vast quantities of gold that would pour from the mine.

The river Lathkill below Over Haddon

However, hardly any gold was found – even deep down. The company was liquidated and many investors were made bankrupt.

⌘ PARWICH

Parwich, a village of some 500 inhabitants, is named in the Domesday Book as Pevrewic and was a royal desmesne. You would not pass through this unusually compact village on your travels in the Peak District – you would have to seek it out. You would be rewarded by a picture postcard limestone village with an intricate pattern of small lanes, ginnels and greens.

Architecturally there are many interesting buildings and in summer the cottage gardens delight the eye with their window boxes and hanging baskets. The church of St Peter replaces the Norman church more than eight centuries old when demolished in 1872. Fortunately the old north doorway and chancel arch have been preserved: over the doorway is an ancient tympanum of very early date

The village of Parwich and the church of St Peter

discovered in the walls of the old church. Parwich Hall, with its magnificent terraced gardens, stands dramatically on the steep hillside, while even higher is the Care Centre built in 1914 as a convalescent home and used as a hospital during the Second World War.

⌘ PEAK FOREST

Peak Forest is set amongst the limestone hills, an attractive village on flat ground in a green bowl. The Royal Forest was founded in 1100 and it was sparsely wooded in some areas, in spite of its name. Wild boar, roebuck and otters were hunted by visiting royalty who stayed at nearby Peveril Castle (in Castleton). In the 16th century, when deer were hunted by settlers and to preserve the remaining herds, a 'park' of about four square miles was enclosed and a house called the Chamber of the Peak was built for the ranger. It was rebuilt in the 18th century and later it became and is now, Chamber Farm. The then Chamber of the Peak was where Swainmotes (forest courts) were held, with a Steward and a small band of foresters.

The clusters of warm stone cottages and farms give a fine background to the church, which was known at one time as the Gretna Green of the Peak. Originally built in 1657 and dedicated to King Charles, King and Martyr, the incumbent of the time was able to grant probate to wills as well as marriage licences. Between the years 1728 and 1754 anyone could come to Peak Forest, day or night, to be married without banns. It was a very busy time there when Bonny Prince Charlie was in the country and a separate register was kept recording these runaway marriages. But in 1804 this register was finally closed by an Act of Parliament. People can still be married in the village without banns, providing that one of the couple has lived there 15 days prior to the ceremony.

⌘ PENTRICH

Pentrich nestles along the side of one of the last hills of the Pennine chain. The Romans came here during the first century, followed eventually by the Saxons and the Normans. In 1152 Pentrich was granted to the Church and remained under canon law until Henry VIII claimed it for the Crown.

The oldest parts of the church of St Matthew date from the reign of King Stephen in 1152, but five Saxon crosses carefully built into the lintels inside the church would seem to indicate that there had been a Saxon church on the site at an earlier time.

The most infamous period of Pentrich history was June 1817 when the Pentrich Revolution made national headlines. Revolution is perhaps too strong a word for what happened when a group of misguided villagers, under the leadership of Jeremiah Brandreth, took up arms in an attempt to overthrow the government. The uprising was meant to include several counties and thousands of men but the few who set off from Pentrich that night were the only ones on the march. They reached the Derbyshire/Nottinghamshire border by dawn the following day, only to be routed by a detachment of Hussars. A much publicised show trial was held in Derby where the three ring-leaders were tried, found guilty of high treason and executed. Fourteen of the other prisoners were transported to Australia.

Pentrich had two social events peculiar to the village. One was the Snowdrop Tea, held on Shrove Tuesday and the other was a Damson Social, held in September to coincide with both the ripe damsons and the patronal festival at St Matthew's church. In the past Pentrich was noted for its damsons. They were grown not for eating but for use as a dye in the textile industry. Many of the old trees still survive but severe winters and strong gales are taking their toll of these brittle old ladies of the hedgerows.

⌘ REPTON

The village lies on the south bank of the river Trent some eight miles from Derby and five from Burton. The Repton brook runs into the Trent here and the Saxon village was built on both sides of the stream, stretching back from the river for about a mile. Its recorded history began about 1,400 years ago when the Mercian royal family established a principal residence at Repton then, following the arrival of Christianity in Mercia in AD 653, a monastery was founded.

The parish church of St Wystan spans the period from the 8th to the 15th centuries, with some later additions. Beneath the chancel is the unique Saxon mausoleum and crypt dating from the early 8th century: among the residents are King Ethelbald of Mercia, King Wiglaf and his grandson, St Wystan.

The village cross and church of St Wystan in Repton

The tall and elegant spire of the parish church (212 ft) is a landmark for miles around – and a tale is told about it: 'There was a steeplejack in Repton in 1804, named Joseph Barton, who was called upon to repair the spire. This he did, watched by an admiring crowd. He received £10, and a goodly collection made among the villagers. He was also given a new suit of clothes. These he took with him when he returned, in a spirit of bravado, to the very apex of the spire. He climbed his ladders as far as possible, then threw up a rope and skilfully hitched it to one of the arms of the cross on top of the spire. He then climbed hand over hand until he reached the bend of the ball, when he crawled up and seated himself at the foot of the cross.

Two or three minutes elapsed during which he was donning the presentation clothes, but at length he stood erect and proceeded to throw into the air, one by one, the discarded garments – the crowd below meanwhile cheering loudly as each garment fell fluttering earthward. Suddenly there was a cry of fright, followed by a deathly hush. The steeplejack had dislodged the rope – his sole connecting link with the earth – and it now hung dangling from the top of his ladder, 30 ft below where he stood. Before anyone could move, his daughter, about 16 years old, went up the tower, then the ladders, rung by rung, until she looked no bigger than a doll. Hanging by her left hand, nearly 200 ft in the air, she threw the rope to her father, and both descended safely.'

⌘ ROWSLEY

Great Rowsley, sitting astride the A6 leading to Bakewell, is one of the gateways to the Peak National Park, as also is Little Rowsley, on the Chatsworth Road.

Great Rowsley has long had strong links with Haddon and with Bakewell. In 1636 Grace, Lady Manners founded a school 'for the better instructing of the male children of the inhabitants of Bakewell and Great Rowsley, in good learning and Christian religion', today's Lady Manners School.

The village with its turnpike gates (two toll-bar cottages still stand) was on a main stage coach route, then in 1849 the railway arrived. A lot of building took place in those years, giving much of the shape of the village today. Not only the railway, with its bridges, viaduct and new station (now gone), but also the school 1840, Wye bridge 1844, the church and vicarage 1855. In the 1890s came the railway houses, the Midland Cottages, with the Methodist chapel in 1910.

Probably the best-known building is the Peacock Hotel, with the inscription above the front door of 'John Stevenson 1652'. It was a one time dower or manor house and farmhouse. In the 19th century Rowsley, 'embosomed in hills', with its thatched houses and two rivers, was the haunt of artists and anglers, who stayed at the Peacock. Mrs Gaskell stayed on a visit to Chatsworth House in September 1857, as did the Emperor Maximillian of Mexico.

Haddon Hall

The village fete takes place during the last weekend in June, with a Well Dressing and Flower Festival in the church, at which time opportunity should be taken to view the tomb, in Siena marble, of Lady John (Catherine) Manners, described by one writer in 1893 as 'the most exquisite monument I ever saw'.

⌘ SCARCLIFFE

Scarcliffe is eight miles south-east of Chesterfield and three miles from the M1 motorway. Most of the land in and around Scarcliffe is owned by the Duke of Devonshire, a group of houses having been built for the Chatsworth estate. There are some fine old buildings in Scarcliffe which are lovingly cared for, and the village still retains its rural character, having been awarded 'Best Kept Village' several times. In recognition of this, trees have been planted in front of the church and along Fox Hill.

The focal point of the village is the church dedicated to St Leonard. It dates from the 12th century, having Norman pillars and a priest's door. Until 1842 the church had a spire, but this was removed and a tower now replaces it. The most well-known part of the church is the tomb of Lady Constantia, an alabaster tomb of mother and child. It is believed that Lady Constantia was one of the de Frechvilles. She and her child were lost in the woods around Scarcliffe when she heard the ringing of a church bell – the curfew bell of Scarcliffe, and made her way towards the sound. In gratitude she bequeathed to the church four acres of land with the proviso that the bells be rung three weeks before and three weeks after Christmas in perpetuity.

⌘ SHARDLOW

Shardlow, recorded in the Domesday Book as Serdelav is a village of contrasts. One is between the speed of the traffic on the A6 and the gentle pace of those travelling on the Trent and Mersey Canal. Another is between the quiet, misty calm of the winter, when the village visitors are mainly anglers and walkers, and

The Trent-Mersey Canal at Shardlow

the bustle of midsummer, when boats travel through the lock in a steady stream and moor along the canal banks, while the pubs and restaurants are full of cheerful holiday makers.

At the crossing on the Trent was Wilden Ferry, a rope-hauled ferry which was replaced in 1760 by Cavendish Bridge. Tolls had to be paid by travellers on the road, which from 1738 was a turnpike and the stone giving the toll charges is still displayed on the roadside, approaching the present modern Cavendish Bridge. This bridge was built in 1956; the old one had collapsed spectacularly one day in the bad winter of 1947.

Then came the canal. Warehouses and wharves were built, ropeworks, saddlers, blacksmiths, ostlers and boat builders were needed to service the horse-drawn boats. Brewers, innkeepers, shopkeepers, clerks and managers organised the traffic and supplied the wants of the boatmen. Small wonder that from 1788 to 1841 the village population quadrupled.

But then the railways came and the canals were too slow for all but the most bulky cargoes, and in 1846 the Shardlow section of the Trent and Mersey Canal was bought by the North Staffordshire Railway. The canal warehouses became grain stores, and other small industries developed such as woodworking and a wireworks.

What can be seen today of Shardlow's past? Many of the old cottages were saved by the designation of much of the canal side as a conservation area in 1978. Shardlow Hall, dating from 1684, is an imposing mansion, now used as offices. It is opposite St James's church, dating from 1839.

⌘ SMALLEY

Smalley is six miles north-east of Derby and has come a long way from its early beginnings. At the time of the Norman Conquest Smael Leah or Smaellage meant narrow clearing – a tranquil spot, surrounded by forest. Smalei is recorded in the Domesday Book in 1086 as having 'a church, a priest and a mill . . .'

A family who helped to shape the history of Smalley was that of the Richardsons. In 1610 they bought the Smalley Farm estate, with coal workings under the local clay. Their descendants prospered as the need for coal grew and the coal was transported to Derby and Leicester. In the early 18th century the brothers John and Samuel Richardson founded a Colliers' Charity, which benefited the village miners, and also endowed a free school for 'twelve poor boys' built in 1721. The endowment continues to this day, though the school is now administered by the local authority.

The parish church houses a chime of five bells. They were given by the Rev Charles Kerry, who was born in Smalley, and whose tomb is in the shade of the ancient yew in the chuchyard. A bell-tower was built to house this gift in 1912. They were brought to the church from the Loughborough bell-founders, garlanded with flowers on a large dray in a procession headed by a band for their consecration. It was only recently discovered that the chime of five bells is the heaviest in England, the largest bell – the tenor – weighing over 40 cwts. The church of St John the Baptist was built in the 18th century on a much earlier site. In the wall of the porch is inserted a 7th century Saxon cross.

⌘ SOUTH WINGFIELD

According to old records, the village was known as Winfeld, the 'winne' being the Old English name for gorse and ling. On Church Lane is the cornmill, dated from the mid 17th century, but there had been a mill of some kind on the site long before this date.

In the churchyard, near the chancel, is a tombstone cover showing a Crusader knight lying cross-legged. This almost certainly belongs to the ancient Norman family of de Heriz, who were lords of the manor of Oakerthorpe. Opposite the churchyard, three brick cottages have now been renovated into one large dwelling. It is thought the priest's house was on this site before the brick cottages and was known as Bakewell Hall. The meadow near to this site is still called Bakewell Meadow.

Field End Cottages, across the road from the Yew Tree inn, were built by the stonemason family of Turners. Their name is carved in the stone lintel over the front door. One member of this family was hanged at Derby, for his part in the doomed 'Pentrich Revolution'. It has been said there is a concealed well in the floor of one room in Field End Cottage; and in despair, the frightened, misled rebels flung their muskets and what other arms they had down it, to conceal their identity when they had been betrayed and were hiding as fugitives.

The railway came to the village in 1835 and was built by George Stephenson. The lord of the manor at that time stipulated that the railway must be at least half a mile away from his Hall, hence the railway station was outside the village. The station buildings were built by Thompson and it was said that Queen Victoria stopped at Wingfield Station and had a cup of tea.

⌘ SPONDON

By the time of the Domesday survey in 1086, Spondon was already a well established agricultural village and so it remained for several centuries. The village was almost completely destroyed by fire in 1340 but through the hard work of the residents Spondon was soon rebuilt and in 50 years also had a huge new stone-built church. Remaining essentially an agricultural village, Spondon grew very gradually until the late 18th century. The Industrial Revolution changed the character of the village – the canal, the railway and heavy industry all brought new residents to Spondon. They in turn brought new money, skills and ideas. The new money meant that new houses were built, especially many larger 'gentleman's residences' for the new professional middle classes. One such is The Homestead, a magnificent red brick Georgian house which stands at the top of Willowcroft Road.

In the 19th century the population trebled; by 1900 it was approximately 2,500 but from then on it just mushroomed. Houses were needed in ever increasing numbers and estates were built by industry, the local authority and private builders. Spondon maintained its popularity as a residential area and that brought about another change to the landscape as several of the larger houses were demolished and replaced by small houses for commuters. In 1968 came the biggest change of all when Spondon was absorbed by the then Borough and became a suburb in the north-east of the now City of Derby.

⌘ STANLEY

Stanley is a pleasantly rural village lying about halfway between the towns of Derby and Ilkeston and sharing a parish with Stanley Common which is about a mile away by winding country lanes.

In the centre of the village stands St Andrew's church, of 12th century origin, but restored and enlarged in 1876. Though small it has an attractive light interior with an interesting carved Jacobean pulpit and screen. There is also a Methodist church in Morley Lane built in 1882.

Off Station Road and bordering Dale Abbey parish is Stanley Grange Farm, one of the oldest and most historically important of the local residences. Parts of the present building originate from the 17th century when neighbouring West Hallam was a Roman Catholic stronghold and the Grange operated as a Jesuit headquarters and boys school. During this period it was the subject of a debate in Parliament and was raided twice by government forces.

Coal mining was once the main industry, as can be seen by the remains of several pits on the outskirts. Drift mining operated at the Footills and evidence can be seen of the longest 'continuous rope' haulage railway which ran from there to Cemetery Hill, Derby. Evidence of past industry can also be seen on either side of Derby Road as it starts to climb the hill out of the village. The sandstone quarry which used to be 100 ft deep is still apparent although now filled in. Originally the stone was quarried for use as a very fine quality polishing stone exported as far away as India. In 1929 however, the enterprising owner, Mr Anthony of Chaddesden, discovered another use for the considerable amount of waste produced and started to manufacture concrete building blocks – the Stanley Building Block. Several houses in the village are constructed of these blocks, and many more may be seen in the Derby suburbs especially Chaddesden and Allenton.

Holy Trinity church, Stanton in Peak

⌘ STANTON IN PEAK

Stanton in Peak is a hillside village, of houses mainly built of gritstone from the Stanton Moor quarries. Also in the parish are Stanton Lees, Pilhough and Congreave, the last two being very small hamlets. The name Congreave means 'rabbit hole', and this is where rabbits used to be kept for the Haddon Hall tables.

Many of the houses date from the 17th and 18th centuries. Holly House was probably built before the window tax of 1697: eight of the 14 windows at the front of the house remain blocked up to this day.

William Pole Thornhill built a good many of the estate houses in the first part of the 19th century; these have the initials WPT in stonework above the door. Around this time the stone quarrying industry thrived, and from a population of 717 towards the end of the century, 103 were employed as quarry workers.

Holy Trinity church has a very unusual feature in that the nave lies from south to north. One of its artefacts is a bronze Italian water stoup from the workshop of Bellini. The church, the school and the reading room were all built by members of the Thornhill family, as was an unusual feature at the side of Coach Lane just beyond Beighton House, and known originally as 'The Belvedere'. This is a viewing platform with a stone seat overlooking the Wye valley, and now referred to as 'The Stand'. The observant walker through the village will notice a number of sturdy stone posts at the side of the streets. These were used to prevent horse-drawn carts from rolling backwards when being unloaded.

⌘ STAUNTON HAROLD

Staunton Harold (Staunton meaning farm on stony ground) is on the border of South Derbyshire and Leicestershire.

Nestling in the centre of a valley of grass and woodland is the Palladian-style Staunton Hall with the beautiful lake in its foreground. Overlooking the Hall stands the church, a superb example of Gothic architecture. It still has its box pews and Jacobean furniture and fittings, and the nave has a painted wooden ceiling representing the Creation. The church is now owned by the National Trust.

The first family to live at the Hall were the Ferrers, later followed by the Shirleys who in the 1700s reverted back to the family name when the title of Earl Ferrers was created.

In 1760 a murder took place at the Hall, when Laurence, the 4th Earl Ferrers, who was separated from his wife, shot his steward, a man called Johnson, after accusing him of administering the estate in favour of the Countess. After a notable trial he was sentenced to be hanged. Dressed in his wedding suit which was embroidered with silver, the Earl was driven to the place of execution in his own landau. He was escorted by a body of constables, horse grenadiers and foot soldiers accompanied by the Sheriff and Chaplain.

In 1955 the estate was dispersed and Group Captain Leonard Cheshire VC, DSO, DFC purchased the Hall and it became one of the famous Cheshire Homes. At the same time, a scheme was approved to build a large dam near Melbourne, and so a large area of countryside between Staunton Park and Melbourne became Staunton Harold Reservoir, which covers 209 acres. The Hall was later purchased by the Sue Ryder Foundation.

⌘ STONEY MIDDLETON

Stoney Middleton nestles among the limestone cliffs and rocks in the beautiful Peak District. It is a village surrounded by stone, and situated on an ancient highway between Chesterfield and Brough. It is mentioned in the Domesday Book as 'Middletune', and Roman coins and a 3rd century bracelet have been found and there were cupolas for smelting lead and lime.

Lover's Leap cliffs at Stoney Middleton

Middleton Dale has always been an awesome place. It is particularly beautiful with its high limestone cliffs and caves attracting climbers and potholers from all over the world. These high limestone rocks are the homes for jackdaws and gilly flowers and each spring the sandmartins return and the cowslips bloom. Also in the Dale is the Lover's Leap so called after a beautiful young local girl named Hannah Baddaley, who in 1760, heartbroken after a lovers tiff, jumped off one of these cliffs. Luckily her dress and petticoats billowed out acting like a parachute, thus saving her life.

The village is full of history. Lord Denman, Lord Chief-Justice of England lived here, lord squire of the Hall. He was a great Victorian reformer, a man with high morals who advocated the abolition of slavery. Lady Denman was the first National chairman of the WI formed in 1917. Denman College now proudly bears her name.

July is well dressing time when the village shares the work and pleasure of dressing three wells in the Nook. The whole village takes part in the many varied activities. After a service of 'Blessing the Wells', and the opening of the festival, the local school children dance round the maypole to a local band. The flower service in church performed by the school children on the Sunday is a delightful custom still carried on, the flowers going to the elderly and sick of the village.

⌘ SUDBURY

Sudbury – meaning South Fortification – has a population of a little under 500, a similar figure to that of 100 years ago. It is situated in the lower valley of the river Dove, within ten miles of the gateway to the Peak District, and is one of the few remaining feudal villages in Derbyshire.

The predominant building is Sudbury Hall, former seat of the Vernon family, now owned by the National Trust. This beautiful house, built during the reign of Charles II, was, for three years, the home of Queen Adelaide, the widow of William IV.

Beyond the Hall, but hidden from view, stands the church of All Saints, which is recorded in the Domesday Book. The east window was given by Queen Victoria and Prince Albert in memory of George Edward Anson, brother of the then rector of Sudbury. The six bells in the tower are rung regularly.

A modern bypass, constructed in 1972, has brought a measure of peace and tranquillity to the largely 17th century village. To the north stands an imposing 18th century deer cote, where herds of deer once roamed in the surrounding parkland.

The sweeping curve of the road through the village is lined on the south side by terraced cottages, their facade of mellow brick little changed since the 19th century.

Sudbury Hall is owned by the National Trust

A 19th century dairy, the first in the country to be subjected to tuberculin tests, sent milk to London twice daily from the adjoining railway station, sadly closed in the late 1950s. The dairy is now a residential home for the elderly.

For the wayward the village provided its own lock-up and stocks; the latter can still be seen and sometimes 'used' by school children visiting the Museum of Childhood at Sudbury Hall.

⌘ SUTTON ON THE HILL

Eight miles to the west of Derby lies the rural village of Sutton on the Hill. As its name suggests, the village is slightly elevated and there are excellent views, particularly of the Peak District. Generally the village is scattered round a number of narrow lanes.

This is a good grassland area and its importance was reflected in the building of a cheese factory in 1876, now converted into houses.

The Domesday survey describing Sutton mentions 'a church and a priest; one mill'. The mill still stands by the brook but ceased to function as a water mill before the Second World War and is now a private house. The dried up mill pond and former watercourses are still clearly visible. The church of St Michael, standing on a hill, was very largely rebuilt in 1863, on its old foundations. The earliest parts of the church are the 14th century arches between the nave and the north aisle and the south wall of the chancel.

The 19th century vicarage, built by the Rev Rowland Ward, was a 'castellated mansion' and must have been quite grand even in the times when vicarages were spacious. This has become the Hall, with its turrets and Gothic appearance, a contrast to the more mundane village architecture. Across a sunken road, lie several fields which are ablaze with daffodils in springtime.

⌘ TADDINGTON AND PRIESTCLIFFE

Taddington is one of the highest villages in England, being 1,000 ft above sea level. Approached by way of the A6 from Buxton via Topley Pike, there is a 1 in 6 hill to

Taddington village is 1,000 ft above sea level

climb and by way of Bakewell through the picturesque Taddington Dale a similar climb along the A6.

Taddington and Priestcliffe are separated by the A6 bypass; the removal of heavy traffic from the main road through the village on to the bypass is a great improvement to village life, but there is always a reminder of bygone days with the old iron London milepost standing at the side of the road.

Taddington is surrounded by pasture land, mainly used for cattle and sheep farming. In the past, the two main industries were lead mining and farming. St Michael's church, part of which was built in the 12th century and rebuilt in the 14th century, has a stone lectern said to be rare beyond Derbyshire, and a 13th century stone font.

Taddington in summertime, with its 17 miles of splendid footpaths, becomes a popular place for ramblers. One of the finest views over the fields and houses, giving a marvellous view of the church, can be seen when dropping down from The Jarnett near Humphrey Gate Quarry (disused) on one side and the children's play area on the other. Many tourists use this point to take photographs of the lovely view.

⌘ TIBSHELF

The village of Tibshelf began as a tiny settlement of nine peasant families around the year AD 800. In the Domesday Book of 1086 it is called Tibecel which is thought to mean 'a place of worship on top of a hill'. Various other spellings have been recorded but the present one has been in use for the past 400 years.

The village had notoriety as a place of one long street, beginning at Overmoor in the east and ending at Nethermoor in the west. Farms and cottages were dotted along this main thoroughfare, widely spaced in the early days, with the gaps being filled in over the years but never much depth of building, and this to a large extent still applies. The church stands centrally on the highest point of this long street and was begun around 1200.

For hundreds of years the economy depended on agriculture, but in 1500 Bess of Hardwick (Hardwick Hall is only two miles away) started a coal mine and this was followed over the years by many others. Then during the 18th and 19th centuries many were employed in framework knitting of cotton hose in their houses, and the noise of the frames could be heard through the village.

In 1553 the Tibshelf estate was given to the Crown as a source of revenue for the newly built St Thomas's Hospital in London, and this unusual landlord continued until the arrival of the National Health Service in 1946.

In recent years British Coal and the local council co-operated in reclaiming the old colliery spoil heaps and unused railway land, creating a network of footpaths and country parks between Tibshelf and surrounding villages. These provide access for the public to enjoy the heritage of natural beauty all around.

Due to its considerable height (about 500 ft above sea level) the village enjoys wonderful views.

⌘ TICKNALL

Ticknall is a picture postcard village on the southernmost tip of the county. It is a village of irregular ribbon development where handsome farmhouses, rosy brick houses and rough hewn stone cottages happily combine.

One famous resident of Ticknall was Mr Edward Moult of Scaddows Farm, known to millions as 'Ted' Moult. He became a popular figure who made it his concern to know and greet by their first names all who lived in the village. At strawberry picking time (he was a pick-your-own pioneer) he would gather up the

St George's church, Ticknall

retired men of the village and leave them on rickety chairs at the field gates in front of a pair of old-fashioned scales to dispense the gleaming fruit.

The comparatively modern church and the ruins alongside share an interesting history. When the population was at its height (1,281 in 1831, about 750 now) it was decided that the existing church of Thomas à Becket was too small. It was demolished and a new larger building erected nearby. The old structure proved very substantial and two fragments, the west wall and altar window, defied contractor's gunpowder and stand now, a silent reproach to an unfortunate decision. The present church has clean lines, mellow stones and a graceful spire. The churchyard is best explored in early spring when snowdrops bloom thickly under the walls, and before summer vegetation has rampaged over the more interesting monuments.

⌘ TIDESWELL

Tideswell lies 1,000 ft above sea level on the limestone plateau of the Peak District. The 14th century parish church of St John the Baptist stands on the site of a 11th century chapelry recorded in the Domesday Book. The patronal festival is celebrated with well dressings, and a week of festivities culminating in a torchlight procession and Morris Dancing, the form and tune of which is unique to Tideswell.

The main occupations in times past have been lead mining, quarrying and agriculture. The village accommodated two velvet cutting mills, while cotton and silk weaving were a cottage industry. Today, quarrying and agriculture survive and a small light industrial estate has been established providing local employment.

Tideswell was once a prosperous market town, with a charter granted in 1250. There were five markets a year for cattle and local produce. This tradition has been revived and is held twice a year, selling local crafts and produce, although no longer cattle! However a Cow Club, founded in 1838, is still active. It originally acted as a form of insurance against veterinary bills and death of cows. It is understood that this club is the only surviving one of its kind.

Oatcakes can still be bought in Tideswell and a few areas in northern Derbyshire. They were staple diet for farm labourers. Many houses had their own 'bakestone'. This was a type of griddle with a fire below to heat the stone. Many housewives baked these fresh in time for breakfast, and they would sell them to eke out their meagre income.

⌘ TINTWISTLE

Dating from Saxon times and referred to in the Domesday survey of 1086, Tintwistle (or 'Tinsel' as it is called) is situated towards the west end of the Longdendale valley on the main Manchester to Sheffield road. It is on the boundaries of Cheshire, Yorkshire, Lancashire and Derbyshire. It has a population of 1,420 inhabitants, with panoramic views of glorious countryside.

There is a legend that Dick Turpin, when pursued by the King's officers after one of his hold-ups, made the village smith, at pistol point, put his horse's shoes on the wrong way about, to give the impression that he was travelling in the opposite direction. This story is not confirmed by any concrete evidence.

Another story related for decades is that of an old travelling sweep, who was found dead on the roadside. He was given a common burial in the churchyard and his clogs were buried with him. It has been said that the trees now growing in that corner of the churchyard sprouted from the wooden soles of his clogs.

Looking through the village of Tissington to the hall

⌘ TISSINGTON

Tissington is a small Derbyshire village which, together with the surrounding land, forms the Tissington estate, where the Hall, which dates from Jacobean times, has been the home of the FitzHerbert family since the 17th century.

The village is known for its well dressings, which is a Christian ceremony to give thanks for pure water and dates back to the time of the Black Death. In years past Ascension Day was looked forward to with great excitement as a large fair arrived each year. The well boards were erected at daybreak on Ascension morning and at one time a young man used to fire a gun at the top of the village to let everyone know it was time to be out of bed.

The railway opened in 1899 with three trains running daily to Buxton and Ashbourne. All the milk, coal and farmers' grains in those days went by train. Passenger services ended in 1954, freight continued until the railway was closed in 1963. Tissington station, once spotlessly kept, became derelict until the Peak Park demolished the old station to make way for the car park for the Tissington Trail.

No building has taken place in the village since 1900 when the baronet had some cottages built for work people, and about this time the railway cottages were built.

The most important building in the village must be the Norman church of St Mary, with many interesting and historic features including the FitzHerbert wall monument.

⌘ TURNDITCH

Turnditch is a small village on the A517 between Belper and Ashbourne. In the Middle Ages this was the ancient forest road linking the two towns. Turnditch is in the valley of the river Ecclesbourne with splendid views towards Wirksworth and Hazelwood.

The church of All Saints was an early chapel of ease, started, it is thought, about 1250, with many later additions. It gained church status in 1847. The stained glass windows on the south side of the nave came from the redundant church of St Werburgh, Derby.

Opposite the church is the village school, a charming listed building. Its original date, 1846, is displayed at the front but the clock tower which gives so much character to the facade was only added in 1910. The school was built on orchard land belonging to a Turnditch farmer, one George Milne. At first there was no room for a playground and the children used the road! Unfortunately several were attacked by a cow passing through the village, causing slight injury.

By 1800 there were two pubs – the Cross Keys and the Tiger, still flourishing today. Hill Cliff (now Lane) was a hamlet in the parish. 'Cross-o-th'-Hands' was the scene, in 1851, of a prize fight watched by 1,000 people when 86 rounds were fought in 95 minutes between contestants who came from Redditch and Nottingham.

⌘ UNSTONE

Unstone and Unstone Green nestle in north-east Derbyshire between Chesterfield and Sheffield. To the north on top of the hill a mile away sit the hamlets of Apperknowle, Summerley, Hundall and West Handley.

Visitors passing through the area today would never guess its history. In 1870 the Midland Railway came through Unstone, for which a very impressive seven-arched viaduct was built. The station was very busy as goods trains carried coal from the local pits and with the prospect of regular work, people flowed into Unstone from as far away as Wiltshire and Suffolk. Unstone became a mining village with spoil heaps dominating the view. However, the last pit closed in the 1930s and after the Second World War miners' dwellings were pulled down or altered, and all that was left were coke ovens almost hidden in the surrounding woods and an enormous tip 369 ft high and covering some nine acres. This was finally removed and used as hardcore under the M1 motorway. A football pitch and community centre now stand on the site.

In the 1820s Unstone Green was known as 'a rough place' and this was confirmed in 1822 when William Twelves set up a Methodist prayer meeting in a thatched cottage in Crow Lane. His first meeting was held behind locked doors while an angry mob tried to break in with an axe. Nevertheless a Methodist church was built in 1847 and thrived for many years until the membership started to decline in the 1960s. In 1977 it finally closed its doors to worship. However, the small congregation were invited by the rector of Dronfield to worship at St Mary's church across the road and so began a very happy relationship between the two congregations.

⌘ WALTON ON TRENT

If you are driving from Staffordshire into the south-west corner of Derbyshire then be careful. You have to cross the Trent at Walton and this is by means of a Bailey bridge which bounces gently even if you walk across it. Anything wider than a big car can be scraped or stuck – as many drivers discover to their cost.

From the Staffordshire bank the village has a traditional look about it: a church amidst scattered houses, with a cricket field alongside. On a gloomy night through mists over the water you might even imagine the ghosts of Celts, Saxons, Danes and medieval figures who all passed here and influenced the place.

No bridge seems to have existed before 1836. Before then there was a ferry, the traditional privilege of ferryman belonging to the landlord of the Black Swan, an inn on the river bank, now replaced by modern houses whose gardens stretch down to the river.

To the south of the present village stands the earthwork known as Borough Hill. This commands an imposing view over the river and is probably the site of an Iron Age fort and the first Walton settlement.

The Domesday survey indicates a village of some 200 people with a priest and church. The present church of St Laurence has some remnants of early Norman building. The first definite record is of the construction of a chantry in 1334 by the rector, Richard Waleys. His tomb and effigy are to be seen there.

The present Walton Hall is a minor stately home built in Georgian style in 1723. Near the Hall is Dripping Pan Cottage. Apparently after the family at the Hall had dined the dripping that remained from their feast was taken in a pan and given to those impoverished labourers living in cottages at the foot of the drive.

⌘ WESSINGTON

Wessington, with a population of approximately 600, is situated on the A615 between Alfreton and Matlock. The heart of the village is clustered around a fairly large green. In days gone by, the green was used for grazing, particularly horses and goats, but in recent years this custom has lapsed and the main users are the Wessington and Ivanhoe football clubs and a group of villagers interested in wildlife conservation who have planted a number of trees. There are three wells on the green and, before the village was able to enjoy mains water, it had to be carried from one of these wells. There are stories of young persons when sent for water for making tea would not make the effort needed to go to the furthest and special Tea Well but would call either at Jubilee Well or Moses Well, whichever happened to be closest to home, and hope that mother wouldn't notice! Jubilee and Moses Well water was used mainly for washing. A young bride really had some hard work ahead of her on washday. First she needed to make numerous visits to the well for water, enough both for washing and rinsing. Then came the pounding of the clothes and boiling nappies over the open fire. After that the dirty water had to be carried out to the nearest drain. The wells are no longer a feature on the green; when no longer needed they were filled in for safety.

⌘ WESTON-ON-TRENT

Weston-on-Trent is a small village of about 500 people which lies seven miles south-east of Derby. Surprisingly for an old village (Weston is mentioned in the Domesday Book) the 13th century church of St Mary the Virgin is situated away from the village near to where the canal now passes, on an elevated site known locally as The Cliff. Buried in the churchyard are two soldiers who were killed in a skirmish at Kings Mills during the Civil War in 1642. The church may also have been used as a look-out post during the Jacobite Rebellion in 1745. The story is that a man was supplied with a musket and instructed to stand on the church tower to defend the people from the army of Bonnie Prince Charlie, which is reputed to have turned back at nearby Swarkestone Bridge.

On the outskirts of the village and close to the church is a Ukrainian Youth Centre used as a campsite by visiting Ukrainians. Also in the grounds, housed in the old rectory, is a Ukrainian old people's home.

The river Trent which forms the southern parish boundary has been navigable from the Humber to Nottingham from earliest times and boats could continue upstream as far as Kings Mill at Weston when there was a sufficient depth of water to enable them to be hauled over the shallows. Following the opening of the canal in the 1770s much waterborne traffic went along the Trent and Mersey Canal, which passes through Weston, taking plaster and alabaster from nearby workings to wider markets. Nowadays the canal is a venue for holidaymakers and fishermen rather than workers.

⌘ WHALEY BRIDGE

Weylech or Weyley, the Anglo-Saxon name for Whaley Bridge, meaning 'the clearing by the road', speaks to us of a time when Macclesfield Forest covered the whole area. Long before this, the Romans had established a crossing over the river Goyt at the spot, on the road they built from Manchester to Buxton. A curious feature of Whaley Bridge, known as the Roosdyche, is a shallow valley about three-quarters of a mile long and with banks on each side. Once believed to have been a racecourse for Roman chariots, research proved it to be simply a glacial valley.

The parish church of Taxal, St James's, was known to be in existence as long ago as 1287 although the church was mostly rebuilt in 1825. It contains an unusual memorial tablet:

'Underneath lyeth the body of Michael Heathcote Esq., Gentleman of the Pantry and Yeoman of the Mouth to His Late Majesty King George the Second, who died June 22nd 1768, aged 75 years.'

Michael Heathcote was born in Taxal but went to live in London on his appointment as the King's 'food taster'. On his death, his remains were returned to Taxal for burial.

The coming of the Industrial Revolution transformed Whaley Bridge: coal mining had always been carried on in the district, but now textile mills sprang up on the banks of the Goyt, a cornmill was established near the old bridge, and an arm of the Peak Forest Canal was extended as far as Whaley, later to be linked to the Cromford Canal by a railway. Today the tide of the Industrial Revolution has ebbedaway from Whaley Bridge but the canal is once more busy with narrowboats – seeking pleasure instead of trade. The reservoir with its wooded

Peak Forest Canal at Whaley Bridge is always busy with narrowboats

slopes is the venue for anglers, yachtsmen and windsurfers, and the network of ancient footpaths and bridleways reaching into the magnificent scenery of the Peak National Park are ever popular with ramblers and riders.

⌘ WHITTINGTON

Whittington, two and a half miles from Chesterfield is reputed to be much older than the Domesday Book's recording of it as Whitintune; a church and rectory are said to have existed since 1140. The original Norman church was replaced by a larger structure in 1865. When this was destroyed by fire in 1895, the tower and bells survived and were incorporated in the new St Bartholomew's which opened the following year.

The Cock and Pynot inn stands at the junction of the old Sheffield and Rotherham road. It was here that in 1688 the plan was devised to bring 'William of Orange and his English wife' to the throne and so depose James II. For his part in the proceedings the Earl of Devonshire was made the first Duke of Devonshire; he later rebuilt Chatsworth House, one of the country's most beautiful ancestral homes. The Cock and Pynot inn, now known as the Revolution House, is a museum of its time. A new Cock and Magpie inn was built nearby.

Richard Dixon commenced making glass in 1710 at Glass House Common. It was to continue for 140 years, 'making a variety of Jacobean drinking glasses both plain and coloured also sturdy dark bottles for storage of wine, sack and ale'. This family were responsible for building Whittington Hall, living there until the business ceased in 1850. After the Dixons, the residence passed through several hands until in 1902 it was leased to Rev Burden for a period of 21 years for use as an Institute for Inebriate Reform, certified to house 50 persons under Home Office licence. By 1912 the character of inmates had changed under the Board of Control to that of 'care of the feeble minded'.

Revolution House, Whittington, is now a museum

⌘ WHITWELL

The Creswell Crags are world famous as a home of early man. These hunters followed the great herds, and their bone carvings are in the British Museum. There are rich remains of animals such as the mammoth, sabre-toothed tiger, and a prehistoric hyena much larger than the present species. Thousands of years later a settlement was mentioned in the Anglo-Saxon Chronicle as Hwitan Wylles Geat; 'the shining stream in the valley'.

A famous son of Whitwell is Charles Edward Wilson. Born in 1853, he became a notable artist, and his paintings were exhibited at the Royal Academy. Several of his studies of Victorian village life are still popular as greetings cards.

The village church of St Lawrence, with its Saxon font and grey stone tower, is central to the village. Two miles away in the hamlet of Steetley the perfect little Norman church featured in Sir Walter Scott's *Ivanhoe* stands in a truly rural setting. The tall chimney of the processing plant of the dolomite quarry represents continuing industry. The dolomite material is crushed and burned, to provide the fireproof lining for blast furnaces.

Before the era of chlorinated pools, generations of Whitwell youngsters learned to swim in the 'Dosh', the stream in the wood. Shutters, kept at a nearby farm, were used to dam the stream. The Ginny Spring provided pure clear water (locals provided the gin). Surface streams are not common in the area, and one wonders if the Saxon Hwitan Wylles Geat was the shining stream in Whitwell Wood, long before the trees were planted.

⌘ WILLINGTON

Willington is situated on the wide, flat fertile gravel plain of the north bank of the river Trent. Its history has been traced back for at least 4,000 years. In 1970 archaeologists discovered the graves of the Beaker People, dated at 2,000 BC. Other artefacts from this dig, now on display in Derby museum, include Bronze Age and Roman pottery.

Willington has always been a convenient crossroads for many forms of transport. Despite the ferry crossing from Meadow Lane across to Tanners Lane in Repton, it is listed in the 1600s as the highest navigable point on the Trent. The port on the river Trent was used for transporting china clay, flints and local cheeses. 1770 saw the building of the Trent and Mersey Canal, with its horsedrawn barges. 1840 brought the Derby-to-Birmingham railway line, and on the far side of the village runs the Derby-to-Crewe line.

Egginton brook, known locally as the Molly, runs through the village and it has provided safe 'jam-jar' fishing for many generations of children. In winter when the mile-wide flood plain surrounding the raised road to Repton is like a lake, the Molly occasionally backs up and overflows.

Creswell Crags prehistoric site

There are very few of the old cottages left. Potlocks Farm, mentioned in the Domesday Book, has a cedar tree. Bargate Lane has a timbered cottage still standing. Perhaps this is where the young man lived who was to marry his sweetheart at a distant church. Having no transport and needing to arise early for his long walk, he made sure of an early alarm call by tying a cockerel to the banister.

⌘ YOULGREAVE

Youlgreave known as Iolograf in medieval times translates as 'Yellow Grove'. It also enjoys the often used local nickname of Pommie, origin unknown.

Youlgreave Well Dressing is regarded as one of the finest examples of the traditional Derbyshire art and takes place at Midsummer each year. Five wells are dressed, all with traditional biblical pictures, and the village plays host to many visitors from all over the country.

Magic and laughter fill the air at least once a year in Youlgreave when the famous pantomime takes to the boards, filling the hall for many performances. Indeed, it was on one such occasion that the bear, grappling with Dame Golightly, mistook his way, and fell off the front of the stage with a resounding crash. A moment's stunned silence and then, picking up its head from under the front row of the stalls and jamming it back on, the bear, Tommy Tomlinson in real life, made his unsteady way to the side door and vanished into the night. Word went round the village that 'that bear from panto' was on the loose, and there were no children seen playing out on the streets after dark for many weeks!